T0268844

MAYA-ENGLISH

ENGLISH-MAYA
(Yucatec)

Dictionary & Phrasebook

DICTIONARY & PHRASEBOOKS

Albanian
Arabic
Arabic (Eastern) *Romanized*
Armenian (Eastern)
Armenian (Western)
Australian
Azerbaijani
Basque
Bosnian
Breton
British
Cajun French
Chechen
Croatian
Czech
Danish
Dari *Romanized*
Esperanto
Estonian
Finnish
French
Georgian
German
Greek
Hebrew
Hindi
Hungarian
Igbo
Ilocano
Irish
Italian
Japanese *Romanized*
Korean

Lao *Romanized*
Latvian
Lithuanian
Malagasy
Maltese
Mongolian
Nepali *Romanized*
Norwegian
Pashto *Romanized*
Pilipino (Tagalog)
Portuguese (Brazilian)
Punjabi
Québécois
Romanian
Romansch
Russian
Serbian *Romanized*
Shona
Sicilian
Slovak
Slovene
Somali
Spanish (Latin American)
Swahili
Swedish
Tajik
Tamil *Romanized*
Thai *Romanized*
Turkish
Ukrainian
Urdu *Romanized*
Uzbek
Vietnamese

MAYA-ENGLISH
ENGLISH-MAYA
(Yucatec)
Dictionary & Phrasebook

JOHN MONTGOMERY

HIPPOCRENE BOOKS, INC.
New York

© 2004 John Montgomery

ISBN: 978-0-7818-0859-0

For information, address:
   Hippocrene Books, Inc.
   171 Madison Avenue
   New York, NY 10016

Book design and composition by Susan A. Ahlquist.

*Cataloging-in-Publication data available from the
Library of Congress.*

Printed in the United States of America.

CONTENTS

INTRODUCTION

When I lecture on Maya culture and Pre-columbian civilization someone almost always asks me what happened to the Maya people. There seems to be a notion among segments of the public that when the civilization vanished, so did the Maya, erased along with their lost world of jungle-shrouded pyramids.

Nothing could be farther from the truth. Approximately ten million Native Americans still speak Mayan, one of the largest continuous blocks of indigenous people on the American continents. Some thirty to thirty-four separate "versions" of Mayan are still spoken over large areas of Mexico, including the modern states of Chiapas, Tabasco, Vera Cruz, Campeche, Quintana Roo, and Yucatán. Mayan is also spoken in the Central American countries of Guatemala, Belize, and Honduras.

The present dictionary and phrasebook offer a selection of the most common words and useful phrases in what linguists generally call Yucatec Maya, probably the largest group of Mayan speakers. The book also includes a broad range of items of interest to travelers, students, and scholars. Spoken over virtually the entirety of Campeche, Quintana Roo, and Yucatán—that is, the Yucatán Peninsula—and isolated areas of Belize, as well as neighboring El Petén in

1

Guatemala, Yucatec Maya constitutes the language generally referred to as "Maya" for historical reasons. Actually "Maya," both culturally and linguistically, derives from a sixteenth-century application of "Mayathan" or "Mayat'aan," meaning literally, "Maya language" (*maya* + *t'aan* "language"). What early Europeans failed to understand was that "Maya" referred to the language spoken by the group of people with whom they were then in contact, and that it bore only an *affinity* with other languages spoken in nearby areas. Each of these languages identifies itself by its own singular name: Quiche, Tzotsil, Tzeltal, and so on. It was linguists who perpetuated the name "Mayan" in reference to all of these related groups.

Strictly speaking, then, "Maya" refers only to "Mayat'aan," the language linguists call Yucatec. For clarity, this book will use "Maya" only for that branch, while identifying others as "Quiche Maya," "Cakchiquel Maya," and so on, with the understanding that "Mayan" refers to the larger language group. The main thing to remember is that **Maya** means Yucatec, **Mayan** the language group as a whole.

To my knowledge, this is the first combination dictionary/phrasebook in Maya/English and English/Maya ever published. (See **Methods of Learning Maya**.) As such, it allows for the use of Maya in most contexts where Spanish would normally be used, although such opportunities are rare for most travelers. Essentially, this book offers "Maya in a nutshell," distilling the essence of the language and focusing on areas of general interest. The goal is to present essential information about the language in the simplest, clearest, and most useful way possible. While a complete explanation of grammar lies outside the scope of the presentation, I do discuss the basic rules—offering something of a "refresher" for those who have experience with the language, making intelligible *why* the language works the way it does for beginners, and as a quick reference. However, a number of complicated issues have been omitted or greatly simplified in the interest of ease of use.

Each Maya word or phrase includes its phonetic pronunciation, plus the *Spanish* equivalent, since most communication in Mexico and Central America takes place in that language. This book assumes some prior knowledge of Spanish, so these entries lack pronunciation guides.

Maya arises out of an incredibly rich cultural tradition, one that holds a great deal of interest for people from outside the Maya world. From ancient pyramids to unique cuisine to personal relationships, many different experiences make this area one of the most interesting in Latin America. It is hoped that the present dictionary and phrasebook will help facilitate those experiences, and promote a more lasting appreciation of Mayat'aan—the Maya language.

A BRIEF HISTORY
OF THE
MAYAN LANGUAGE GROUP

ANCIENT AND WRITTEN MAYAN

Archaeologists have found evidence of farming villages on the Yucatán Peninsula dating back to at least 1200 B.C., and we know that even before that date primitive hunter-gatherers foraged for jungle and coastal resources. Whether these were Mayan speakers remains uncertain. Linguists argue that, based on sound changes among the various branches of Mayan, there was a single dominant language as early as 2000 B.C., called Proto-Mayan, which began to evolve into several major divisions not long afterwards. Yucatec, or "Maya," emerged as a separate branch of this larger language family by around 1000 B.C. Today the "Yucatecan" branch includes Yucatec proper, or Maya, as well as Lacandon, Itzá, and Mopan. Certainly Yucatec Maya has a continuous history of at least three thousand years.

Mayan speakers created the high Precolumbian civilization of the Classic Period, which flourished from about A.D. 250 to 900. Whatever dialect they spoke, they were responsible for perhaps the greatest intellectual achievement of Native American history—the invention of a fully developed written script, or Maya hieroglyphic writing. While scholars long have believed the glyphs record predominantly a Cholan Maya language, speakers of Yucatec Maya were writing in books made from bark paper when Cortés and his Spanish conquistadors arrived in the early sixteenth century, and the closely related Itzá Maya were still maintaining books as late as 1697. Clearly, Mayan—written in its own native system—has a longer history than either written English (eighth century A.D.) or Spanish (eleventh century A.D.).

Following the Spanish conquest, a few Mayan speakers wrote their language with European characters, producing works of epic literature and "chronicles." The manuscripts known as the books of *Chilam Balam* constitute some of the best-known literature of the latter type, detailing great epochs in Maya history. This series of documents was widely published in both Spanish and English translations. In more recent years, epigraphers, or decipherers of hieroglyphs, have reintroduced to native speakers the original hieroglyphic system, a renaissance taken up with alacrity by speakers of different branches of the Mayan language group.

NAHUATL AND SPANISH LOANWORDS

With the collapse of Classic Maya civilization in the ninth and tenth centuries A.D., widespread cultural change took place throughout Precolumbian America. Eventually the Aztec empire emerged as the most powerful civilization in Precolumbian history. Speakers of the Aztec language, which is called Nahuatl, ranged far down the coasts of Honduras and Panama. They were mostly traders and merchants who brought various social changes and introduced features of material culture.

Even before this a variety of peoples had penetrated the Maya area from central Mexico and elsewhere, establishing political control in some cases over local populations. Overall, what resulted were sundry "borrowings" from the Mexican Nahuatl language (or one of its variants), as well as intermarriage between these distinct groups of people.

Through Nahuatl new personal names were introduced to the Maya, as well as words for things and places (for example, *máasewáal* "Indian, Maya," from Nahuatl *macehuali*, "free commoner").

Spain's conquest of the New World in the sixteenth century inevitably destroyed much of Native American civilization, and although ferociously resistant, the Maya also succumbed. With the wholesale introduction by the conquerors of new foods, methods of cooking, clothing, weapons, and social and political institutions, the Maya were forced to adapt in different ways. They did so not least by employing Spanish words for things of which they had no experience, and even for some familiar things. Examples include *asukaar*, from the Spanish *azúcar* "sugar," *áamigoh* from the Spanish *amigo* "friend," and *paapah*, from the Spanish *papá* "father."

Spanish continues to encroach on the Maya world (and almost as importantly, English now does so as well). Most Maya men have to be bilingual because of contacts beyond their villages, and they can switch back and forth between Spanish and their own language in the middle of conversation, a process called code-shifting. However, pronunciation of Spanish tends to be

"Mayanized" by lengthening the vowels, changing the location of accents, adding the characteristic Maya singsong tonality and pitch, and substituting Maya sounds for Spanish ones not found in Maya. At the same time Maya speakers retain traditional Spanish pronunciation for technical terms. In particular, Spanish proper and personal names remain a prominent feature of today's spoken Maya.

Modern Maya

Ancient Maya and Colonial Maya from the sixteenth and seventeenth centuries differ considerably from Modern Maya, and many terms and conventions regularly used in the past have fallen away. Moreover, because modern Maya for the most part remains a *spoken* language as opposed to a written one, and because speech constantly changes and adapts, Maya lacks uniformity among its several million speakers. There really is no such thing as "pure Maya" or "standard Maya." The historical tendency of the Maya to seek isolation and independence led to numerous "sub-dialects," and just about every Maya has his or her own way of speaking. Regional variations exist as well. Speakers of Maya can readily understand each other (although not necessarily other branches of Mayan such as Quiche or Tzotsil), but the situation poses some difficulty for speakers of Maya as a foreign language. Changes in the language from one village to another and from one area to the next can be very confusing for the beginner.

METHODS OF
LEARNING MAYA

As with any language, the process of learning Maya may seem at first overwhelming. Unfamiliar sounds can strike the ear of the beginner as impossibly complex, especially when spoken rapidly. Difficulty in distinguishing where one word begins and another ends can hopelessly confuse the student, even a vigilant one.

In contrast, like languages everywhere around the world, Maya becomes far easier to learn when the student listens and familiarizes his- or herself with the sound of the language. Familiarity breeds affinity, even endearment, with the spoken language, while the mind's inner ear and subconscious quietly absorb what we learn, often with much greater depth than the conscious mind realizes. The true seat of language belongs to the subconscious, which stores information about language very much like an automated dictionary and grammar.

Anyone interested in learning Maya can choose from several approaches, depending on what goal he or she has in mind. An informal conversational command of Maya for personal reasons probably can best be achieved through "total immersion." On the other hand, a more scholarly interest might require formal classroom instruction or the use of language tapes. Certainly all serious students will master spoken Maya most thoroughly by availing themselves of every resource that time and money allow.

TOTAL IMMERSION

To totally absorb the language, the student should visit the Yucatán Peninsula and live among the Maya for as extended a period as possible. Total immersion involves living, eating, and sleeping with a Maya family. Daily routine and habitual exposure to the language "immerses" the student in all things Maya. Such an approach probably offers the quickest and most surefire way to learn the language, but will probably cost more than other methods. Generally students can simply approach individual Maya or their families and hire them as teachers. Language schools, usually operated out of Mérida, often place students with Maya families to supplement one-on-one instruction through trained teachers.

ONE-ON-ONE FORMAL EDUCATION

Probably the second quickest (and second most reliable) method involves the pairing of students with a native Maya speaker who acts either as an informal teacher or trained instructor. Usually language academies offer this kind of instruction, generally in Mérida but also elsewhere on the peninsula. Virtually any Maya speaker willing to teach will suffice, although professionally trained teachers often prove more valuable for students seeking academic knowledge of the language.

Formal Classroom Instruction

Highly efficient but more formally organized and structured than either total immersion or one-on-one contact with an instructor, formal classroom instruction offers an extremely valuable resource, especially when conducted by native speakers or where native speakers serve as teacher assistants. A main disadvantage is that students may not receive enough personal attention or may fail to keep up with the classroom pace. Duke University provides the best-known program, conducted for four weeks during the summer months through the Institute of Latin American Studies. The program offers an optional two-week field school with one-on-one instruction and total immersion, conducted on the Yucatán Peninsula.

Language Tapes/CDs

Language tapes offer a key tool for anyone wanting to learn Maya. They allow students to listen to and learn Maya outside the classroom and without live native speakers. With this method, personalized learning can take place in a variety of settings, for example, while driving an automobile or in the privacy of the home. Currently only one complete audio language course exists, *Spoken (Yucatec) Maya* by Robert Blair and Refugio Vermont-Salas, which was produced in the 1960s. A xeroxed transcription of the tapes can be ordered separately from the University of Chicago Library (Microfilm Collection of Manuscripts on American Indian Cultural Anthropology, numbers 65–66, Series X). The tapes are available from the University's language library.

DICTIONARIES

Dictionaries and grammars provide crucial resources for any student, and students should develop a reference library with as many published and privately printed resources as possible. Gary Bevington's *Maya For Travelers and Students: A Guide to Language and Culture in Yucatan* (University of Texas Press, Austin, 1995) provides the most valuable and accessible compendium of modern Maya, including Maya-to-English and English-to-Maya dictionaries. Bevington's volume also comes with a separate language tape that provides introductory material, although the tape and dictionary are sometimes packaged together. *A Dictionary of the Maya Language As Spoken in Hocabá, Yucatan*, compiled by Victoria Bricker, Eleuterio Po'ot Yah, and Ofelia Dzul de Po'ot, offers another extensive if academic resource (University of Utah Press, Salt Lake City, 1998). Many additional locally published dictionaries can be found in bookstores in Mérida and other towns on the peninsula, although these usually provide Maya-to-Spanish entries.

The best approach that any student can take is to combine the above resources into one systematic course of study. Accordingly, anyone seriously interested in learning Maya should live with native speakers while undertaking one-on-one instruction, and then should follow with formal classroom instruction and the regular use of language tapes.

PRONUNCIATION AND SPELLING GUIDE

Maya and other members of the Mayan language family use letters from the Spanish alphabet, omitting ones for which Mayan has no sounds and adding combinations of letters for the Mayan sounds that Spanish lacks. However, at the time of the Spanish conquest Spanish itself lacked consistency or even rules for basic punctuation, and a large degree of variation resulted. Modern linguists transcribing Maya into English compounded the problem.

Worse, today's spelling conventions among speakers of both Maya and Spanish vary tremendously. Spanish alone presents something of a nightmare; consider alternative spellings of "cow"—*vaca* versus *baca*—or Jiménez versus Ximénes. (Even English includes similar and confusing spellings or pronunciations, as for example "cock," meaning "rooster," versus the appelative "Coch" or "Koch").

The problem increases exponentially with Maya, because certain sounds have no equivalent either in Spanish *or* English. A survey of dictionaries and maps turns up a confused array of spellings, as in *ts'ib*, *tz'ib*, and *dzib* for the word "writing."

Recently, native language academies have introduced a uniform alphabet, a system taken up by decipherers of Maya hieroglyphs and exemplified in the massive Maya/Spanish dictionary published in Mexico, known as the *Cordemex*. Although often used inconsistently, the system has an advantage of fairly wide acceptance. The present dictionary follows the *Cordemex* with the exception that it retains traditional spellings for personal and place names used in the Maya area and on maps (for example, Dzibalchaltun instead of Tz'ibalchaltun), and it distinguishes long and short vowels.

GLOTTAL STOPS

Like the click sounds made in certain African languages, the "glottal stop" poses a distinct problem for non-native speakers. In the alphabet used to write Maya, ' represents the sound made in stopping the breath which is similar to the stoppage of air in English *uh-oh* or in *button* when spoken rapidly. Pronounced simultaneously with the vowel or consonant that it accompanies, the glottal stop gives a characteristic "pop" to the sound.

Glottal stops might pose little problem if they carried no meaning, but the distinction between *kab* (without the stop) and *k'ab* (with the stop) represents an important difference. The one means "bee," the other "manual labor." This is similar to the difference between *sweet* and *sweat* in English. The glottal stop changes *everything*.

Any vowel can be glottalized, but Maya includes only five glottalized consonants where the glottal stop changes the meaning.

ch'   k'   p'   t'   tz'

Linguists sometimes glottalize other consonants, for example *b'*, but these make no difference in meaning. The present dictionary ignores the glottalization of consonants except the five listed above.

VOWELS

Maya uses the same vowels as Spanish, but distinguishes between long and short ones. Lengthening the vowel changes the meaning of a word. The present book *doubles* long vowels when these make a difference in meaning, for example *ka'* "two" versus *kaa'* "again." Short vowels should be pronounced as follows:

A   The sound of *a* in "father"
E   The sound of *a* in "fate"
I   The sound of *ee* in "feet"
O   The sound of *o* in "go"
U   The sound of *o* in "who"

Long vowels incorporate a system of tonality that differentiates meaning. The present dictionary renders high-toned long vowels by adding an accent over the first vowel, while it leaves low-toned long vowels unmarked—for example, *áa* ("high" tone) and *aa* ("low" tone).

CONSONANTS

Maya employs nineteen consonants, with all but six consonants pronounced like their Spanish counterparts. Note that Maya lacks *d*, *f*, or *v*. For the most part *r* remains exceptionally rare.

B   Sounds like the *b* in "bed" but somewhat softer between vowels; often weak or unpronounced at the ends of words

CH   The sound of *ch* in "church"

CH'   The sound of *ch* in "church" but with breath-stream stopped at the same time

H   Unlike *h* in Spanish, which is always silent; instead, sounds like English *h* in "house"; but unlike English it can occur before other consonants, as in *hmeen* "shaman"

K   Sounds like English hard *c* in "caught" or "cat"

K'   Sounds like English hard *c* but with breath-stream stopped at the same time

L   Like Spanish or English *l* but often weak or unpronounced at the ends of words

M   Like Spanish or English *m*

N   Like Spanish or English *n*

P   Like Spanish or English *p*

P'   Like Spanish or English *p* but with the breath-stream stopped at the same time

S   Like Spanish or English *s*

T   Like Spanish or English *t*

T'   Like Spanish or English *t* but with the breath-stream stopped at the same time

TZ	Sounds like *ts* in English "let's" or "toots"
TZ'	Like *ts* in English "let's" but with breath-stream stopped at the same time
X	Sounds like English *sh* in "shoe"
W	Like Spanish or English *w*
Y	Sounds like English *y* in "yes"

SYNCOPATED VOWELS AND CONSONANTS

In certain instances when adding suffixes to verbs, Maya drops unglottalized short vowels in the middle of words, not unlike English when adding "-ing" to *sicken* or *label*, which results in *sickning* and *labling*. In a variation of this, long vowels become shortened, depending on the sounds that follow. In these instances *aa* becomes *a*. Words with *b* and *l* at the end regularly drop these consonants. However, in certain words the final *b* and *l* and long vowels with an internal glottal stop (for example *e'e*) *must* be pronounced. In addition, in normal to rapid speech native speakers of Maya often ignore glottal stops.

STRESS AND INTONATION

Modulation of tone and pitch gives Maya a marked singsong quality best learned by imitation. This rhythmic, melifluous characteristic makes Maya one of the most attractive Native American languages spoken today. In general, three types of observations can be made regarding pitch and tone:

1) Pitch rises toward the ends of words
2) Vowels last or second to last rise in pitch in many words
3) The long vowels in some words, even towards the beginning of the word, form a "peak" in overall pitch

SPELLING CONVENTIONS USED FOR VOWELS IN PRONUNCIATION GUIDES

In the Maya-English Dictionary, English-Maya Dictionary, and Phrasebook sections of the present book, the pronunciation guides (given in parentheses after individual Maya words and sentences) use the following conventions to represent vowels.

a   =   ah (pronounced as in the English exclamatory expression "ah!")
        Example: **sak** (sahk)

aa =   aah (pronounced as "ah" but with vowel elongated)
        Example: **saak'** (saahk')

áah =   áah (pronounced as "aah" but with initial á raised in tone)
        Example: **sáal** (sáahl)

e   =   eh (pronounced like "ay" in English "pay")
        Example: **kex** (kehsh)

ee = eeh (pronounced as "eh" but with vowel
       elongated)
          Example: **beel** (beehl)

ée = éeh (pronounced as "eeh" but with
       initial é raised in tone)
          Example: **kéeh** (kéeh)

i   = ee (pronounced as in the English word
       "see")
          Example: **pik** (peek)

ii = eee (pronounced as "ee" but with vowel
       elongated)
          Example: **piitz'** (peeetz')

íi = éee (pronounced as "ee" but with initial
       é raised in tone)
          Example: **píim** (péeem)

o   = oh (pronounced as in the English
       exclamatory expression "oh!")
          Example: **toh** (toh)

oo = ooh (pronounced as "oh" but with vowel
       elongated)
          Example: **toon** (toohn)

óo = óoh (pronounced as "ooh" but with
       initial ó raised in tone)
          Example: **t'óon** (t'óohn)

u   = oo (pronounced as in the English word
       "zoo")
          Example: **lu'** (loo')

uu = ooo (pronounced as "oo" but with vowel
           elongated)
                Example: **luuk'** (loook')

úu = óoo (pronounced as "oo" but with initial
           ó raised in tone)
                Example: **lúub** (lóoob)

ABBREVIATIONS

adjective	adj.
adverb/adverbial	adv.
auxiliary	aux.
completive	com.
conjunction	conj.
demonstrative	dem.
English	Eng.
first person	1st p.
imperative	imper.
incompletive	incom.
interrogative	inter.
intransitive	in.
noun	n.
participle	par.
phrase	phr.
plural	pl.
preposition	prep.
pronoun	pron.
reflexive	refl.
second person	2nd p.
singular	s.
Spanish	Sp.
third person	3rd p.
transitive	tr.
verb	v.

OVERVIEW OF MAYA GRAMMAR

Sentence Structure

Sentences with subjects only (intransitive): In Maya the subject can either lead or follow the verb or predicate, but most commonly in Maya the subject follows the verb. Hence an intransitive sentence is either VERB-SUBJECT (VS) or SUBJECT-VERB (SV).

English: *As for John, he is sleeping.*
Maya: either
  Juane' táan u wenel (SV)
  or
  táan u wenel Juan (VS)

Sentences with both object and subject (transitive): As in intransitive sentences, the subject in transitive sentences can either lead or follow the verb, with the object placed after the verb. In Maya, however, the subject most commonly follows both the verb and object. Hence, most transitive sentences are VERB-OBJECT-SUBJECT (VOS).

English: *John saw Peter*
Maya: either
  Juane' tu yilah Pedro
  or
  Tu yilah Pedro Juan
  (equivalent to *saw Peter John*)

Placing the subject before the verb *highlights* the subject, with the highlighted subject often presented as new information.

VERB FORMS

Verbs express action. Maya has three basic verb forms (transitive, intransitive, and passive), plus three aspects (completive, incompletive, and subjunctive). For purposes of simplification the discussion ignores both passive and subjunctive forms. Overall, Maya includes four qualities that need to be taken into consideration when forming verbs: 1) transitive/intransitive; 2) completive/incompletive; 3) singular/plural; and 4) first, second, or third person. In addition, most verb forms have three basic elements of construction: 1) a verb root that includes a postfix differentiating transitivity as well as aspect; 2) usually an auxiliary verb; 3) and pronominal affixes (prefixes, suffixes, and infixes).

While sentence structure depends on the presence of a subject or object, verbs incorporate root words that must be inflected depending on whether the verb is transitive (subject plus object) or intransitive (subject only).

han	=	eat
tin hanal	=	I am eating (intransitive)
tin haantik	=	I am eating it (transitive)

Aspect

Aspect can be thought of more or less as tense in English or "time relationships." Affixes that indicate aspect depend on whether the action is completed at the time of the utterance (completive) or ongoing (incompletive; resembles the infinitive in English). For all intents and purposes Maya lacks a "future tense," but the future can still be expressed through the use of the auxilliary verb *he'el* "will."

Completive: Can be thought of essentially as past tense, in other words as a *finished* action.

tin haantah le waaho' = I ate that tortilla

Incompletive: Indicates an action that either was or is ongoing, not unlike the English infinitive where the verb ends in *-ing*. Also used with verbs where the activity is repetitive or habitual.

tin haantik waah = I was/am eating tortillas

Pronominal Affixes

Pronouns differentiate person and number, as in "I/we said it" (first person), "you said it" (second person), and "he/she/they said it" (third person). Maya incorporates three distinctive sets of pronouns: Set A, Set B, and Set C. These are attached either to the verb stem or to another component of the sentence.

Set A:

Pronouns from Set A, called the "Ergative Set," mark the subjects of transitive verbs and the possessors of nouns. "Ergative" refers to the function of the pronoun to indicate the agent or instrument of an action (the subject).

When singular pronominal affixes from Set A precede a root word beginning with a vowel, the root takes *w* prefixed to it after the pronouns *in* or *a*. However, if a word already begins with a vowel and calls for the third-person pronoun *u*, the third-person pronoun affix changes to *y* and the initial vowel of the root is often dropped (both with verbs and possessed nouns).

u baak	=	his/her bone
yotoch	=	his/her house

The following table lists the various pronouns from Set A in singular and plural forms. Note that pronoun forms can both begin and end the root, the latter indicated by —.

	Singular	*Plural*
1st person	*in*	*k*
		in—o'on
		k—e'ex
2nd person	*a*	*a—e'ex*
3rd person	*u*	*u—o'ob*

Set B:

Also called the "Absolutive Set," Set B consists exclusively of pronominal affixes attached to the end of the verb root (as opposed to those in Set A, which can occur both at the beginning and end). Set B pronouns occur with some incompletive transitive constructions and with completive intransitives to mark the subject.

The following table lists the various pronouns from Set B.

	Singular	Plural
1st person	-een	-o'on
2nd person	-eech	-e'ex
3rd person	-ih*	-o'ob

*Technically not a pronoun but rather the completive marker. Present when the pronoun marks the subject and the verb is the last word in the sentence. Otherwise the third-person singular has a "silent" marker (f), or an "invisible" and unpronounced affix.

Set C:

Pronouns from Set C use pronouns from Set B, but combine these with the preposition *ti'*, meaning "to" (*ti'* also means at, in, on, and with).

	Singular	Plural
1st person	*teen* ("to me")	*to'on*
2nd person	*teech* ("to you")	*te'ex*
3rd person	*leeti'* ("to him/her") *ti'e* ("to him/her")	*leeti'o'ob* *ti'o'ob(e)*

Incompletive Intransitives

In addition to pronominal inflection, an incompletive intransitive verbal construction will take the suffix -v*l*, where "v" stands for a changeable vowel and *l* provides the final consonant. When the verb is simple, rather than complex, then vowels used in the final -v*l* suffix reflect the same vowel used in the root word. Otherwise v = *a*. Incompletive intransitives also take an "auxiliary," a wide variety of which may be used. Two variations of intransitive verbal constructions distinguish this category: 1) Set A pronoun affix > stem > suffix (relatively rare); and 2) auxiliary > Set A pronoun > stem > suffix.

1st Person:
Singular

k	> *in*	> *han*		-*al*
aux.	1st p. s.	verb stem		> incom. in.
	Set A	"eat"		suffix

Translation: *kin hanal* "I eat"

Plural

k	> *in*	> *han-al*	> -*o'on*
aux.	1st p. s.	verb stem "eat"	1st p. pl.
	Set A	+ incom. in. suffix	Set A

Translation: *kin hanalo'on* "we eat"

Plural (alternate)

k	>	*han-al*	> -*e'ex*
aux.		verb stem "eat"	1st p. pl.
		+ incom. in. suffix	Set A

Translation: *k hanale'ex* "we eat"

2nd Person:
Singular

k	> a	> han-al
aux.	2nd p. s.	verb stem "eat"
	Set A	+ incom. in. suffix

Translation: *ka hanal* "you eat"

Plural

k	> a	> han-al	> -e'ex
aux.	2nd p. s.	verb stem "eat"	2nd p. pl.
	Set A	+ incom. in. suffix	Set A

Translation: *ka hanale'ex* "you all eat"

3rd Person:
Singular

k	> u	> han-al
aux.	3rd p. s.	verb stem "eat"
	Set A	+ incom. in. suffix

Translation: *ku hanal* "he/she eats"

Plural

k	> u	> han-al	> -o'ob
aux.	3rd p. s.	verb stem "eat"	3rd p. pl.
	Set A	+ incom. in. suffix	Set A

Translation: *ku hanalo'ob* "they eat"

Thus the inflectional paradigm of incompletive intransitives may be characterized as:

Singular	*kin hanal*	=	"I eat"
	ka hanal	=	"you eat"
	ku hanal	=	"he/she eats"
Plural	*kin hanalo'on*	=	"we eat"
	k hanale'ex		
	k hanal		
	ka hanale'ex	=	"you all eat"
	ku hanalo'ob	=	"they eat"

Incompletive Transitives

Verbs marked as incompletive transitives take the suffix *-ik* plus an auxiliary verb, in addition to Set A and Set B pronouns, where Set B pronouns can be added to the end of the verbal construction or to mark the object.

1st Person:
Singular

k	> in	> *hatz'*	-ik
aux.	1st p. s.	verb stem	> incom. tr.
	Set A	"hit"	suffix

Translation: *kin hatz'ik* "I hit it/him/her" (periodically in the present)

Plural

k	> *hatz'*	> ik	> -e'ex
aux.	verb stem	incom. tr.	1st p. pl.
	"hit"	suffix	Set A

Translation: *k hatz'ike'ex* "we hit it/him/her"

Plural (alternate)

k	>	in	>	hatz'		>	-ik	>	-o'on
aux.		1st p. s.		verb stem			incom. tr.		1st p. pl.
		Set A		"hit"			suffix		Set A

Translation: *kin hatz'iko'on* "we hit it/him/her"

2nd Person:
Singular

k	>	a	>	hatz'	>	-ik
aux.		2nd p. s.		verb stem		incom. tr.
		Set A		"hit"		suffix

Translation: *ka hatz'ik* "you hit it/him/her"

Plural

k	>	a	>	hatz'		>	-ik	>	-e'ex
aux.		2nd p. s.		verb stem			incom. tr.		2nd p. pl.
		Set A		"hit"			suffix		Set A

Translation: *ka hatz'ike'ex* "you all hit it/him/her"

3rd Person:
Singular

k	>	u	>	hatz'	>	-ik
aux.		3rd p. s.		verb stem		incom. tr.
		Set A		"hit"		suffix

Translation: *ku hatz'ik* "he/she hits it/him/her"

Plural

k	>	u	>	hatz'		>	-ik	>	-o'ob
aux.		3rd p. s.		verb stem			incom. tr.		3rd p. pl.
		Set A		"hit"			suffix		Set A

Translation: *ku hatz'iko'ob* "they hit it/him/her"

To specify exactly who or what was hit in all of the above examples, simply add a name or noun phrase at the end, as in *kin hatz'ik Juan* ("I hit Juan") and *ku hatz'ik le pak'o'* ("She/he hits the wall"). You can also add the Set B pronouns (except *-i*) to the end of these forms, except that the singular/plural markers must not be doubled. Examples of the latter include *kin hatz'ikeech* "I hit you," and *ka hatz'ikeen* "you hit me."

The inflectional paradigm of incompletive transitives may be characterized as:

Singular	kin hatz'ik	=	"I hit it"
	ka hatz'ik	=	"you hit it"
	ku hatz'ik	=	"he/she hit it"
Plural	kin hatz'ike'ex	=	"we hit it"
	k hatz'iko'on		
	k hatz'ik		
	ka hatz'ike'ex	=	"you all hit it"
	ku hatz'iko'ob	=	"they hit it"

Completive Intransitives

Completive intransitive verbal constructions require no auxiliary, but they take Set B pronouns to mark the subject. All that completive intransitives require is the verb root and a Set B suffix.

1st Person:
Singular

han	>	-een
verb stem		1st p. s.
"ate"		Set B

Translation: *haneen* "I ate"

Plural

han	> -o'on
verb stem	1st p. pl.
	Set B

Translation: *hano'on* "we ate"

2nd Person:
Singular

han	> -eech
verb stem	2nd p. s.
	Set B

Translation: *haneech* "you ate"

Plural

han	> -e'ex
verb stem	2nd p. pl.
	Set B

Translation: *hane'ex* "you all ate"

3rd Person:
Singular

han	> -ih
verb stem	3rd p. s.
	Set B

Translation: *hanih* "he/she ate"

Plural

han	> -o'ob
verb stem	3rd p. pl.
	Set B

Translation: *hano'ob* "they ate"

The inflectional paradigm of completive intransitives may be characterized as:

Singular	haneen	=	"I ate"
	haneech	=	"you ate"
	hanih	=	"he/she ate"

Plural	hano'on	=	"we ate"
	hane'ex	=	"you all ate"
	hano'ob	=	"they ate"

Completive Transitives

Just as incompletive intransitives take the suffix -al and incompletive transitives the suffix -ik, so too completive transitives add the suffix -ah. They also use the auxiliary t-, together with Set A pronouns, while Set B pronouns mark the object.

1st Person:
Singular

t	> -in	> hatz'	> -ah
aux.	1st p. s.	stem	com. tr.
	Set A	"hit"	suffix

Translation: *tin hatz'ah* "I hit it" (in the past)

Plural

t	> hatz'	> -ah	> -e'ex
aux.	stem	com. tr.	1st p. pl.
		"hit"	Set A

Translation: *t hatz'ahe'ex* "we hit it" (in the past)

Plural (alternate)

t	> -in	> hatz'	> -ah	> -o'on
aux.	1st p. s.	stem	com. tr.	1st p. pl.
	Set A	"hit"	suffix	Set A

Translation: *tin hatz'aho'on* "we hit it" (in the past)

2nd Person:
Singular

t	> a	> hatz'		> -ah
aux.	2nd p. s.	stem		com. tr.
	Set A	"hit"		suffix

Translation: *ta hatz'ah* "you hit it" (in the past)

Plural

t	> a	> hatz'	> -ah	> -e'ex
aux.	2nd p. s.	stem	com. tr.	2nd p. pl.
	Set A	"hit"	suffix	Set A

Translation: *ta hatz'ahe'ex* "you all hit it" (in the past)

3rd Person:
Singular

t	> u	> hatz'		> -ah
aux.	3rd p. s.	stem		com. tr.
	Set A	"hit"		suffix

Translation: *tu hatz'ah* "he/she hit it" (in the past)

Plural

t	> u	> hatz'	> -ah	> -o'ob
aux.	3rd p. s.	stem	com. tr.	3rd p. pl.
	Set A	"hit"	suffix	Set A

Translation: *tu hatz'aho'ob* "they hit it" (in the past)

The inflectional paradigm of completive intransitives may be characterized as:

Singular	*tin hatz'ah*	=	"I hit it"
	ta hatz'ah	=	"you hit it"
	tu hatz'ah	=	"he/she hit it"
Plural	*t hatz'ahe'ex*	=	"we hit it"
	tin hatz'aho'on		
	ta hatz'ahe'ex	=	"you all hit it"
	tu hatz'aho'ob	=	"they hit it"

Subjunctive Verbs

Subjunctive verbs appear in the context of subjective, doubtful, hypothetical, or grammatically subordinate statements and are thought of as expressing a mood of uncertainty. For simplification, the present dictionary and phrasebook avoids subjunctive entries.

Subjunctive Transitive: Set A pronominal affix followed by the transitive verb stem, with Set B pronouns suffixed when required as object pronouns.

Subjunctive Intransitive: Intransitive verb stem followed by the suffix -vk, with "v" determined by the vowel of the stem, followed in turn by a Set B pronominal suffix except when third person singular.

Subjunctive Passive: Transitive verb stem followed by the suffix -*a'ak*, together with Set B pronominal suffix.

Passive Verbs

Verbs rendered in the passive voice indicate that the subject of the sentence undergoes the action of the verb, without direct reference to an object, as in the English example, "the ball is carried." For all intents and purposes the present dictionary and phrasebook avoids entries in the passive voice.

Passive Completive: Transitive verb stem marked by the suffix -*ab*, with pronominal suffix from Set B added as subject.

Passive Incompletive: Transitive verb stem with the suffix -*a'al*, prefixed by the optional auxiliary *tan* and Set A pronominal affix *in*.

"Irregular" Verbs

Maya incorporates special classes of verbs that must be conjugated in ways that differ from the paradigms given above. For example, not all incompletive intransitive verbs take the -*vl* ending, although otherwise they are inflected according to the regular pattern. Such verbs add a suffix to the stem before adding any Set B pronouns, with the suffix commonly consisting of a consonant followed by -*ah* (as in -*nah*). Exceptions include the verbs *bin* "go" and *taal* "come," as in *tin bin* "I am going," and *taleen* "I came."

Another class of "irregular" verbs consists of intransitives ending in -*tal*, which express a meaning of "becoming" or the process of getting to a particular state or condition. Examples include *sáastal* "become light" and *nóokoytal* "become overcast." In the completive *-chah* replaces the *-tal* suffix, and Set B pronouns are added, as in *kalchaheech* "you got drunk."

Auxiliaries

Auxiliaries consist of a wide variety of supplemental elements that mark incompletive transitive, completive transitive, and intransitive verbs. When verbs take auxiliaries, a Set A pronoun always immediately follows the auxiliary form. Sometimes auxiliaries contract or combine with the following pronoun, not unlike the contraction in English of words such as "can't" (for "can not").

táan: Denotes activities as processes, like the progressive *-ing* form in English. Sometimes, but not always, contracts in the following ways:

táan in	=	*tin*
táan a	=	*tan*
táan u	=	*tun*
táan k	=	*tank*

Example: *tin haantik waah* "I'm eating tortillas"

k: Kind of a "default" auxiliary of vague meaning and origin. Common in questions that ask for information. Also used in sentences describing habitual or repeated action.

tu'ux ka bin	=	"where do you go?"
ba'ax ka wa'alik	=	"what did you say?"
Juane' ku konik si'	=	"John sells firewood"

ma': The negative particle meaning "no" or "not." Negative sentences end in *-i'*, so that *ma'_____i'* almost always frames the verb stem.

ma' + in	=	*min*
ma' + a	=	*ma'*
ma' + u	=	*mu'*
min woohli'	=	"I don't know"
mu'k'ahoteeni'	=	"she/he doesn't recognize me"

taak: Expresses desire. Never contracts with the pronoun.

taak in kanik le maya't'aano'	=	"I want to learn Maya"

ho'op'/hok': An "inceptive" auxiliary meaning to initiate or begin something. Can be used, along with appropriate endings, as a regular verb. *Hok'* serves as an auxiliary variant in Quintana Roo.

ho'op' u hanal	=	"she is beginning to eat"

k'abéet: An auxiliary that indicates necessity or obligation.

k'abéet in áantik le nohoch máako'	=	"I've got to help that old man"

yan: An auxiliary that expresses need or necessity, but associated with volition and intention. Often an expression of future time. In addition, *yan* has a completed form—*yanhi*—used as an equivalent to the English "had to."

yan in áantik le nohoch máako'	=	"I'm going to help the old man"
		"I should help the old man"
yanhi in áantik le nohoch máako'	=	"I had to help the old man"

tz'ok: A "terminative" auxiliary that focuses attention on the end or completion of something. Used with incompletive verb forms although it focuses on the "end" of something. Sometimes contracts with the singular pronoun from Set A, and can be used with *k* "we."

tz'in
tz'a
tz'u

tz'ok in hanal	=	"I'm done eating"
tz'ok in k'atik	=	"I've already asked for it"

Stative Verbs

Stative verbs express states of being, as in *ke'eleen* "I am cold." Not all verbs that express states function as statives, but rather, statives function as the equivalent of adjectives in English or Spanish. In addition, nouns can be converted to stative verbs, as with *wíinik* "I am a man" (*wíinik* = "man, person"), and some statives can be used to form sentences all by themselves, for example *ke'eleen* "cold/I am cold." Statives can also have associated subjects:

k'oha'an	=	"sick"
k'oha'an Juan	=	"sick is John"
Juane' k'o'ha'an	=	"John is sick"

To speak about "I, we, you," and so forth, simply add the appropriate Set B pronoun:

k'oha'aneen	=	"I am sick"

"Have" Verbs

Speakers of English use the word "have" to inquire about things, as in "do you have any money?" In Maya, as in Spanish, the speaker also inquires about something by asking about its existence in conjunction with the "have" verb *yaan*: *yaan teech taak'in?* "do you have any money?" When the thing inquired about involves alienable possession, as with things that can be disposed of by sale, abandonment, or loss, *yaan* combines with a C Set pronoun (*yaan + ti'—o'ob*).

NOUN PHRASES

Noun phrases, consisting of the subject phrase dominated by a noun, take additional elements that modify the subject. Determinatives, which consist of articles and elements that substitute for articles, function as the most basic set of noun modifiers, and include demonstratives (this/that) and possessives (my/your). Other modifiers include:

Prepositions and Prepositional Phrases

Locatives: Include the all-purpose preposition in Maya, *ti'*, and indicate general direction or location: to, from, in, on, at. When the article *le* or pronominal affixes *in*, *a*, or *u* follow *ti'*, typically in their possessive function, the two contract: *te*, *tin*, *ta*, and *tu*. In addition, Set C pronouns resemble contractions of *ti'* with Set B pronouns, as in *teen* "to me," *teech* "to you," *te'ex* "to you" (plural), *to'on* "to us," *leeti'* "to him/her," and *leeti'o'ob* "to them." To express "to him/her/it" you use *ti'* by itself, marked with clause-final *-e'* tacked on:

ti'e'	=	"to him/her"
ti'o'ob(e)'	=	"to them"

Other prepositional forms include:

yéetel	=	"with"
uti'a'al	=	"for"
yóok'ol	=	"over, above"
yáanal	=	"under"
tu	=	"beside"
chúumuk	=	"in the middle"

Plurals

As with Spanish and English, plural forms in Maya take a single suffix, in this case *-o'ob* (*che'* "tree," versus *che'o'ob* "trees"). However, when context makes it obvious that something involves more than one thing, the plural marker may be dropped (as in the imperative *áak! "turtle!"* when, for example, sighting a bevy of turtles along the beach). The word for "tortilla" (*waah*) never takes the plural suffix, and as a rule, nouns are rarely pluralized after numbers and quantifiers.

Demonstratives

Demonstratives emphasize a noun, as in the English examples "the tree," "this tree," and "that tree." The most common Maya demonstrative simply adds the determinative article *le* to the beginning of the noun and the suffix *-o'* at the end.

le che'o'	=	"that tree"
le che'o'obo'	=	"those trees"

To say "this" or "these" simply add *-a'* instead of *-o'*:

le che'a	=	"this tree"
le che'o'oba'	=	"these trees"

To say "a" or "an" (as in English "a tree" or "an hour"), add *hun* "one" before the noun together with a numerical classifier (something that marks the counting of or number of a particular class of things, for example to mark animate versus innanimate things). Indefinite plurals lack an article.

| *hunkúul che'* | = | "a tree" |
| *che'o'ob* | = | "trees" |

Possessives

Nouns take Set A pronouns to form the possessive, and *-il* or *-vl* may be added as an optional suffix, where "v" stands for "vowel" and corresponds to the vowel of the noun stem.

nah	=	"house"
in nahil	=	"my house"
a nahile'ex	=	"your (pl.) house"

Special rules apply to possessives. The *-il/vl* suffix comes before any other suffix. In addition, the plural suffix always precedes the *-e'ex* part, as in *nahilo'be'ex* "your (pl.) houses." Lastly, only one *-o'ob* suffix can be used, as in *u nahilo'ob*, which serves to designate "his/her houses," "their house," and "their houses." Some nouns are always possessed, for example, body parts and family relatives: *a ni'* "your nose" and *a taatah* "your father." Names or descriptive nouns that possess something take *u* as prefix and sometimes the *-il/vl* suffix, together with the name of the possessor: *u nahil Juan* "John's house." *U* can also be used to form the equivalent of English "of":

chúumuk	=	"middle"
u chúumuk	=	"its middle"
u chúumuk le kaaho'	=	"the middle of town"

Requests

Forms that express requests, or imperatives, differ for transitive and intransitive verbs. Transitives include simply the verb stem, with all aspectual suffixation stripped away. Sometimes *e* and *h* can be added.

tasik	=	"bring" (incom. t.)
tas ten hump'éel	=	"bring me a (cup of)
síis ha'		hot water"
hanteh	=	"eat it" (from *haantik*)
chupeh	=	"fill it" (from *chupik*)

Intransitives are formed by removing any aspectual suffix and adding the imperative suffix *-en*.

hanal	=	"eat"
hanen	=	"eat!"

Request forms of *bin* and *taal* become *xen* "go" and *ko'oten* "come." All command forms can be pluralized by adding *-e'ex*: *ko'otene'ex* "you all come."

Questions

Questions in Maya generally incorporate words that end in *x* and that occur at the beginning of a sentence. The primary exception is the word *máakalmáak*, meaning "which?"

ba'ax	=	"what?"
máaxi	=	"who?"
bix	=	"how?"
tu'ux	=	"where?"

The word *kux* serves to ask the same question a second time but about a different person or object.

ba'ax taak a uk'ul?	=	"what do you want to drink?"
kux teech?	=	"and you?"

Phrase Markers

Phrase markers bracket or sandwich a noun or a noun and an adjective.

Le + -o' or *-a'*:

le peek'o'oba'	=	"these dogs"
le nukuch peek'o'obo'	=	"those big dogs"

Ma' + -i':

ma' in woohli'	=	"I don't know"
min woohli'	=	"I don't know"

Discourse Markers

Suffix *-i'*:

Tacked onto the end of question words when these are used alone:

ba'ax	=	"what?"
ba'axi'	=	"what is it?"

Suffix *-e'*:

Added to the subject to "focus" the subject when it appears before a verb.

Juan tun wenel	=	"John is sleeping"
Juane' tun wenel	=	"as for John, he's sleeping"

Suffixes *-ih* and *-e'* used as "terminals":
Function like punctuation marks at the end of verbs, and include *-e'* after the preposition *ti'* (*ti'e'* "to him") and *-ih* after completive intransitives (*binih* "he went").

QUANTIFIERS

Quantifiers consist of words used to express relative amounts. They may or may not include a plural marker, in which case the quantifier appears redundant.

ya'ab	=	"a lot," "much"
ya'ab ha'	=	"a lot of water"
ya'abach	=	"many"
ya'ab máak	=	"a lot of people"
ya'abach máak(o'ob)	=	"many people"

NUMERICAL CLASSIFIERS

When counting something, numbers take special suffixes called "numerical classifiers." Classifiers differ depending on what the speaker counts. For example, *-p'éel* follows the number when counting inanimate things, *-tz'íit* follows when counting slender, long things, *-kúul* follows when counting trees, and *-túul* follows when counting people or animals.

If *hun* "one" and *kan* "four" take the classifier *-p'éel*, then the *n* in the stem word changes to *m* (for example, *hump'éel*).

The use of numerical classifiers has declined over the years, and many Maya speakers simply use the *-péel* suffix with all inanimate objects, rather than using *-kúul* and *-tz'íit.*

MAYA-ENGLISH DICTIONARY

A

a (ah) *SetA pron.* second-person singular; second-person plural together with suffix **-e'ex**

áabil (ÁAH-beel) *n.* grandchild; *nieto*

aach (aahch) *n.* spur, goad, sting; *espuela, ramal, picadura*

aak (aahk) *n.* grass; *yierba*

áak (áahk) *n.* turtle; *tortuga*

áakan (ÁAH-kahn) *n.* snort, bellow, groan; *bufido, gemido*

áaktun (ÁAHK-toon) *n.* cave; *cueva*

aak' (ahk') *n.* tongue; vine; *lengua; bejuco*

áak' (áahk') *adj.* fresh, green (immature); *fresco, verde (immaduro)*

áak'ab (ÁAHK'-ahb) *n.* night; *noche*

áak'abtal (áahk'-AHB-tahl) *in. v.* to become night; *anochecer*

aak'al (AAHK'-ahl) *n.* lagoon, spring, swamp, tank, reservoir; *laguna, ciénega, pantano, tanque, embalse*

áak' bak' (ÁAHK' bahk') *n.* fresh meat; *carne fresco*

aak'nal (AAHK'-nahl) *n.* green corn; *maíz verde*

áak'sa' (ÁAHK'-sah') *n.* green corn gruel, fresh maize gruel; *atole de maíz tierno, atole nuevo*

aal (aahl) *n.* son, daughter; weight; *hijo, hija; peso*

aalak' (AAHL-ahk') *n.* pet, domestic animal; *animal doméstico*

aalak'tik (aahl-AHK'-teek) *tr. v.* domesticate, grow; *criarlo, crecerlo*

áalkab (ÁAHL-kahb) *in. v.* run, do something very fast; *correr, hacer algo de prisa*

áalkab meyah (ÁAHL-kahb MEHY-ah) *in. v. phr.* work rapidly; *trabajar muy rápido*

aal k'ab (aahl k'ahb) *n.* finger; *dedo*

aalnook' (AAHL-noohk') *n.* doll; *muñeca*

aal ook (AAHL oohk) *n.* toe; *dedo de pie*

áamigoh (áah-MEE-goh) *n.* friend; Sp. loanword; *amigo*

aanis (AAHN-ees) *n.* commercial cane liquor;
  Sp. loanword; *anís, aguardiente*

aantah (AAHN-tah) *n.* helper; *ayudante*

áantah (ÁAHN-tah) *in. v.* help; *ayudar*

áantik (ÁAHN-teek) *tr. v.* help; *ayudarlo*

aanyo (AAHN-yoh) *n.* year; Sp. loanword; *año*

aasta (AAHS-tah) *prep.* until; Sp. loanword; *hasta*

aax (aahsh) *n.* wart; *verruga*

áayin (ÁAHY-een) *n.* crocodile, caiman, alligator;
  cocodrilo, caimán

abal (AHB-ahl) *n.* plum; *ciruela*

ahal (AH-hahl) *adj.* awake; *despierto*

ahal (AH-hahl) *in. v.* awaken; *despertarse*

ahal (AH-hahl) *tr. v.* awaken; *despertarlo*

ak (ahk) *adj.* last; *último*

ak' (ahk') *n.* clitoris; *clítoris*

alux (AH-loosh) *n.* forest spirit, guardian of a cornfield;
  duende del bosque, guardián de la milpa

am (ahm) *n.* spider; *araña*

asben/asbe'en (AHS-behn/AHS-beh'-ehn) *adj.*
  secondhand, used; *de medio uso*

asukaar (ah-SOO-kaahr) *n.* sugar; Sp. loanword; *azúcar*

atan (AH-tahn) *n.* wife; *esposa*

awat (AH-waht) *n.* shout; *grito*

ay (ahy) general expression of pain or disgust; *¡ay, dios!*

ayik'al (ahy-EEK'-ahl) *adj.* rich, wealthy; *rico*

a'al(ik) (AH'-AHL-[eek]) *tr. v.* say, tell; *decir*

B

baab (baahb) *n.* piece (continuous); *pedazo (continuo)*

báab (báahb) *in. v.* swim; *nadar*

baach (baahch) *n.* chachalaca (bird, *Ortalis vetula*);
  pájaro que se llaman chachalaca

baak (baahk) *n.* bone; horn; *hueso; cuerno*

báalam/balan (BÁAH-lahm/BAH-lahn) *n.* jaguar;
  jaguar; tigre

báalche' (BÁAHL-cheh') *n.* fermented honey beer,
  flavored with bark; *balche*

baanda (BAAHND-ah) *n.* area, place; *banda, lugar*

báat (báaht) *n.* ax, hatchet; *hacha*

baatz' (baahtz') *n.* monkey (howler); *mono chillón, saraguate*

báaxal (BÁAHSH-ahl) *in. v.* joke, play; *bromear, jugar*

báaxal (BÁAHSH-ahl) *tr. v.* amuse; *entretener, divertir*

báaxal t'aan (BÁAHSH-ahl T'AAN) *n.* joke, pun; *chiste, retuécano*

báaxtik (BÁASH-teek) *tr. v.* play, toy with; use; *jugarlo; usarlo*

bab (BAHB) *n.* crab; *cangrejo*

babahkil (BAHB-ahk-eel) *adj.* crowded; inflamed; stocked (well-); *atestado; hinchado; bien surtido*

bakal (BAHK-ahl) *n.* corncob; *hueso del maíz, tusa (de maíz)*

bak' (bahk') *n.* meat; *carne*

bak'el iit (BAHK'-ehl EEET) *n.* buttock, rump; *nalga*

bat (baht) *n.* hail; *(piedra de) granizo*

ba'al (bah'-ahl) *n.* thing; *cosa*

ba'alche' (BAH'-AHL-che') *n.* animal (wild); *animal silvestre, bruta, bestia*

ba'ate'/ba'ate'el (BAH'-AH-teh'/ BAH'-AH-teh'-ehl) *n.* fight; problem; *pelea; problema*

ba'ax (BAH'-ahsh) *inter.* what?; *¿qué?*

ba'ax k'iin (BAH'-ahsh K'EEEN) *inter.* when (what day)?; *¿cuándo (qué día)?*

ba'ax oorah (BAH'-ahsh OOHR-ah) *inter.* when (what hour)?; *¿cuándo (qué hora)?*

ba'ax ten (BAH'-ahsh-tehn) *inter.* why?; *¿por qué?*

beech' (beehch') *n.* quail; *codorniz*

beel (beehl) *n.* affair, matter; road; *asunto; camino*

beetik (BEEH-teek) *tr. v.* do, make; *hacer*

beey wale' (beehy WAHL-eh') *adv.* perhaps it is so!; *¡tal vez es posible!*

behla'ak (BEH-lah'-ahk) *adv.* earlier today, today (earlier); *hoy anteriormente*

behla'(e') (beh-LAH'-[eh']) *n.* nowadays, today; *hoy*

bek'ech (BEH-k'ehch) *adj.* slender, thin; *delgado*

beooráah (beh-OOH-ráah) *adv.* immediately; Sp. loanword; *en seguido*

beya' (BEH-yah') *adv.* like this; *así*

beyo' (BEH-yoh') *adv.* like that; *así*

bíix (béeesh) *inter.* how?; *¿cómo?*

bin (been) *in. v.* go; *irse*

bin ka ak'abtal (been kah AHK'-ahb-tahl) *n.* dusk,
  sunset; *anochecer*
bis(ik) (BEES-[eek]) *tr. v.* take; *llevarlo*
bolon (BOH-lohn) (hypothetical) *n.* nine; *nueve*
bonik (BOHN-eek) *tr. v.* paint; *pintarlo*
bóoch' (boohch') *n.* shawl; *rebozo, chal*
book (boohk) *n.* odor, smell; *olor*
boon (boohn) *n.* dye, paint; *tinta, pintura*
boonol/bo'on (BOOHN-ohl/BOH'-ohn) *adj.* painted;
  pintado
bóox (bóohsh) *n.* lips; *labios*
box (bohsh) *adj.* black; *negro*
boxha' (BOHSH-hah') *n.* coffee; *café*
bo'ot(ik) (BOH'-OHT-[eek]) *tr. v.* pay (for); *pagarlo*
bo'ox (BOH'-ohsh) *n.* buttocks; *nalgas*
bo'oy (BOH'-ohy) *n.* shade, shadow; *sombra*
buluk (BOO-look) (hypothetical) *n.* eleven; *once*
but'ik (BOOT'-eek) *tr. v.* pack, stuff, fill; *embutirlo,*
  llenarlo
buuh (booo) *n.* owl; possible Sp. loanword; *búho*
  (tecolote)
búukintik (bóoo-KEEN-teek) *tr. v.* dress, put on
  clothes; *vestirse, ponerlo ropa*
buutz' (boootz') *n.* smoke; *humo*
bu'ul (BOO'-ool) *n.* bean; *frijol*

CH

cháak (cháahk) *n.* rain; *lluvia*
chaampal (chaahm-PAHL) *n.* baby, child; *niño/niña, bebé*
chaanbeel (CHAAHN-beehl) *adj.* slow; *despacio, lento*
chab (chahb) *n.* anteater; *oso hormiguero*
cha(ik) (CHAH-[eek]) *tr. v.* allow, permit; *permitirlo,*
  dejarlo
chak (chahk) *adj.* red; *colorado, rojo*
chakik'at (chahk-EEK'-aht) *n.* hurricane, cyclone;
  huricán, ciclón
chakmo'ol (chahk-MOH'-OHL) *n.* jaguar (*Felis onca*);
  jaguar, tigre
chaknul (chahk-NOOL); *adj.* naked; *desnudo*
chakpose'en (chahk-poh-SEH'-ehn) *adj.* pink; *rosado*
chakxich' (CHAHK-sheech') *adj.* blond; fair; *güero*
chan (chahn) *adj.* little, small; *pequeño, chico*

chan ch'eel (CHAHN ch'eehl) *n.* redheaded child, blond child; *niño güero*

cha' (chah') *tr. v.* free, loosen, release, allow, let; *dejar libre, desatar, soltar, dejar, permitir*

cha'an (chah'-ahn) *n.* spectacle, show; *espectáculo*

cheba (CHEHB-ah) *n.* beer; *cerveza*

cheem (cheehm) *n.* canoe; boat; washtub; *canoa; barco; cuba de lavar*

che' (cheh') *n.* pole, stick; wood; tree; *palo, vara; madera; arbol*

che'eh (cheh'-eh) *n.* laughter; *risa*

che'eh (cheh'-eh) *in. v.* laugh; *reírse*

chich (cheech) *adj.* strong; tough; *fuerte; duro*

chichan (CHEECH-ahn) *adj.* little, small; *pequeño, chico*

chichiik' (CHEECH-eeek') *n.* hurricane, storm; *huracán, tempestad, temporal*

chiich (cheeech) *n.* grandmother; *abuela*

chiinah (CHEEE-nah) *n.* orange (sweet); *naranja dulce*

chiinah pah (CHEEE-nah PAH) *n.* orange (sour); *naranja agria*

chiin wol (CHEEEN wohl) *n.* tarantula; *tarántula*

chikoop (CHEE-koohp) *n.* bat (vampire); *murcielago de vampiro*

chik'in (CHEE-k'een) *n.* west; *oeste, occidente, poniente*

chilankabil (chee-lahn-KAHB-eel) *n.* relative; *pariente*

chiltal (CHEEL-tahl) *in. v.* lie down; *acostarse, echarse (en el suelo)*

chi' (chee') *n.* edge; mouth, opening; *orilla; boca*

chi'ibal (CHEE'-EE-bahl) *in. v.* bite; hurt; *morder; doler*

chi'ik (chee'-eek) *n.* coatimundi (*Nasua narica yucatanica*); *coatimundi*

chi'ikam (CHEE'-EE-kahm) *n.* jicama (edible plant); *jícama*

chokoh (CHOHK-oh) *adj.* hot; *caliente*

chokokúuntik (choh-koh-KÓOON-teek) *tr. v.* heat; *calentarlo*

chokotal (chohk-oh-TAHL) *in. v.* become hot; *calentarse*

chokwil (CHOHK-weel) *n.* fever; *calentura*

chooch (choohch) *n.* intestines; *intestinos, tripas*

chowak (CHOH-wahk) *adj.* long; *largo*

chowakil (CHOH-wahk-eel) *n.* length; *largura, longitud*

chuka'an (CHOO-kah'-ahn) *adj.* captured; *capturado*

chukbesik (CHOOK-beh-seek) *tr. v.* complete, finish; *completarlo, terminarlo*

chukik (CHOOK-eek) *tr. v.* catch; attain; *alcanzarlo; pescarlo*

chukpachtik (chook-PACH-teek) *tr. v.* overtake, pursue, catch up with someone; *alcanzar, alcanzar él que va adelante, alcanzar alguien*

chunchumuk (choon-CHOO-mook) *adj.* fifty-fifty; *mitad y mitad*

chunpahal (choon-PAH-hahl) *in. v.* get started; *empezarse, comenzar*

chupik (CHOOP-eek) *tr. v.* fill; *llenarlo, hincharlo*

chúuh (chóooh) *n.* bottle gourd (*legonaria siceraria*), canteen; *calabaza para llevar agua, calabaza vinatera*

chúuk (chóook) *n.* charcoal; *carbón*

chúuka'an (CHÓOOK-ah'-ahn) *adj.* complete, finished; *completo, terminado*

chúumuk (CHÓOOM-ook) *n.* center, middle; *centro, medio*

chúumuk áak'ab (CHÓOOM-ook ÁAHK'-ahb) *n.* midnight; *media noche*

chúumuk k'iin (CHÓOOM-ook K'EEEN) *n.* noon; *media día*

chuun (chooon) *n.* base, stem, trunk; beginning, origin; *raíz, principio, tronco; origen*

chuunik (CHOOON-eek) *tr. v.* begin; *empezarlo, comenzarlo*

chuup (chooop) *adj.* full, swollen; *lleno, hinchado*

chuupul (CHOOOP-ool) *adj.* filled; *hinchado*

chuuy (choooy) *in v.* sew; *costurar*

CH'

ch'aik (CH'AH-eek) *tr. v.* seize, take; use; *agarrarlo, llevarlo; usarlo*

ch'akik (CH'AHK-eek) *tr. v.* cut with a blow; *cortarlo con un golpe*

ch'amak/ch'omak (CH'AH-mahk/CH'OH-mahk) *n.* coyote; fox; *coyote; zorro*

ch'a'iik'/ch'aik iik' (CH'AH'-eeek'/CH'AH-eek EEEK') *tr. v.* breathe; *respirar*

ch'eel (ch'eehl) *adj.* fair; blond; redheaded; *güero; rubio; pelirrojo*

ch'eel (ch'eehl) *n.* magpie; *urraca*

ch'e'eh (ch'eh'-eh) *adj.* noisy, loud; *ruidoso, bullicioso*

ch'e'en (CH'EH'-ehn) *n.* cistern, well; *cisterna, pozo*

ch'iha'an (CH'EE-hah'-ahn) *adj.* old; *viejo*

ch'íich' (ch'éeech') *n.* bird; *ave, pájaro*

ch'iih (ch'eeeh) *tr. v.* make old, age; *hacer viejo*

ch'iihil (CH'EEE-eel) *adj.* grown; *crecido*

ch'ilib (CH'EEL-eeb) *n.* toothpick; twig; *palillo de dientes; ramita*

ch'inik (CH'EEN-eek) *tr. v.* throw; throw stones (at); *tirarlo; tirar piedras a*

ch'oom (ch'oohm) *n.* vulture; buzzard; *zopilote; busardo*

ch'óop (ch'óoohp) *adj.* blind; *ciego*

ch'óoy (ch'óohy) *n.* bucket; *cubeta, cubo*

ch'o' (ch'oh') *n.* mouse; rat; *ratón; rata*

ch'uhuk (CH'OO-hook) *adj.* sweet; *dulce*

ch'uhuk (CH'OO-hook) *n.* candy; *dulce*

ch'ukik (CH'OOK-eek) *tr. v.* loosen; wrinkle; *desatar; arrugarse*

ch'ul chahtal (ch'ool CHAH-tahl) *in. v.* become wet; *mojarse*

ch'ulik (CH'OOL-eek) *tr. v.* moisten; drench; *mojarlo; remojarlo*

ch'úuk (CH'ÓOOK) *in. v.* spy; *espiar*

ch'uul (ch'oool) *adj.* moist, wet; *mojado*

ch'úuyul (CH'ÓOOY-ool) *in. v.* hang (fruit); *colgarse fruta*

ch'uytal (CH'OOY-tahl) *tr. v.* hang, suspend; *colgarlo*

ch'u' (ch'oo') *n.* epiphyte; *espilladero, epífita*

E

eek' (eehk') *n.* star; *estrella*

éek' (éehk') *adj.* dirty; black; *sucio; negro*

éemel (ÉEHM-ehl) *in. v.* descend; *bajarse*

éensik (ÉEHN-seek) *tr. v.* lower; *bajarlo*

éet (éeht) *aux. v.* equal; same; *igual; mismo*

eex (eehsh) *n.* pants; underwear; *pantalón; calzón*

ée'hoch'e'en (éeh'-HOHCH'-eh'-ehn) *adj.* dark; *oscuro*

eh (eh) *n.* file, edge; *filo*

elel (ehl-ehl) *in. v.* burn; *quemarse, arderse*

e'esik (EH'-EHS-eek) *tr. v.* show; *mostrarlo*
e'esk u bah (EH'-EHSK oo BAH) *refl. v.* show oneself;
    mostrarse

H

h (h) nominal honorific denoting masculine names, he
    of; *honorífico denotando nombres masculinos, él de*
haah (haah) *adj.* true; *verdadero*
haah (haah) *adv.* yes; *sí*
haahil (HAAH-eel) *n.* truth; *verdad*
háal (háahl) *n.* base; edge, side; *raíz; orilla*
haaleb (HAAHL-ehb) *n.* paca, spotted cavy (kind of
    rodent, *cuniculus paca*); *tapescuintle*
háanil (HÁAHN-eel) *adj.* clean, clear (of objects);
    limpio
haantik (HAAHN-teek) *tr. v.* eat; *comerlo*
haay (haahy) *adj.* thin (paper, clothes); *papel o ropa*
    delgado
háay (háahy) *adj.* cloak, cape (article of clothing);
    napkin; *capa; servilleta*
hach (hahch) *adv.* very; *muy*
hach k'aas u bin (HAHCH k'aahs oo BEEN) *adj.*
    dangerous; *peligroso*
hach ya'ab (HAHCH yah'-ahb) *adj.* a lot, much;
    enough, too much; *mucho; bastante*
hach'ik (HAHCH'-eek) *tr. v.* chew; *mascarlo*
hahalkil/hoholkil (hah-hahl-KEEL/hoh-hohl-KEEL)
    adj. slippery, smooth; *liso, resbaloso*
hak'óolal (hah-K'ÓOHL-ahl) *adj.* surprising,
    frightening; *sorprendente, con susto*
hanal (HAHN-ahl) *n.* food, meal; *comida*
hanal (HAHN-ahl) *in. v.* eat; *comer*
hatzik (HAHTZ-eek) *tr. v.* divide; diminish; leave; take
    away; *dividirlo, partirlo; disminuir; dejarlo; quitarlo*
hatzkab k'iin (hahtz-kahb K'EEEN) *adv.* early;
    morning; *temprano; la mañana*
hatz'ik (HAHTZ'-eek) *tr. v.* beat, hit, whip, strike;
    golpearlo, azotarlo, pegarlo
hatz'utz (HAHTZ'-ootz) *adj.* beautiful, nice, very good;
    hermoso, bonito, bello, muy bien
hatz'utzil (HAHTZ'-ootz-eel) *n.* beauty; goodness;
    belleza; bondad

hayk'inta'an (hahy-K'EEN-tah'-ahn) *adj.* dried; *seco*

hayk'intik (hahy-K'EEN-teek) *tr. v.* dry (in the sun); *secarlo en el sol*

ha' (hah') *n.* lake; rain; water (in general); *laguna; lluvia; agua (en general)*

ha'ab (hah'-ahb) *n.* year; *año*

ha'abil (u) (HAH'-AHB-eel [oo]) *n.* age; *edad*

ha'as (hah'-ahs) *n.* banana; *plátano*

heban/he'an/he'ik (heh-BAHN/heh'-AHN/heh'-EEK) *adj.* open; *abierto*

hebik (heh-BEEK) *tr. v.* open; *abrirlo*

heeb (heehb) *in. v.* open; *abrirse*

heel (heehl) *adj.* different; other; *diferente; otro*

hela'an (HEH-lah-ahn) *adj.* different, distinct, strange; *diferente, distinto, extraño*

hetz'a'an (HEHTZ'-ah'-ahn) *adj.* firm, seated, secured, fixed, settled; *firme, sentado, asegurado, fundado*

he' (heh') *n.* egg; *huevo*

he'el(a')/(o') (HEH'-EHL-a'/o') *dem.* here/there it is!; *aquí/allí está* (a' = close, o' = further away)

he'elel (heh'ehl-EHL) *in. v.* rest; *descansar*

he'ele' (HEH'-EHL-eh') *adv.* indeed, yes, to be sure; *sí, claro*

he'e máax (heh'-eh MÁAHSH) *pron.* whoever, anyone; *quien, cualquier persona*

he'esik u ba (HEH'-EHS-eek oo bah) *refl. v.* rest oneself; *descansarse*

he' u beeta'ale' (heh' ooh BEEH-tah'-ahl-eh') *adj.* possible (if); *si se puede*

hmeen (ah-MEEHN) *n.* herbalist, shaman, curer; *yerbatero, curandero*

hochik (HOHCH-eek) *tr. v.* harvest; *cosecharlo*

homa' (HOH-mah') *n.* gourd (large); *calabaza/jícara grande*

hooch (hoohch) *in. v.* harvest; *cosechar*

hóok'ol (HÓOHK'-ohl) *in. v.* come out; go, leave; *manifestarse; salir*

hool (hoohl) *n.* entrance; hole, opening; *entrada; hoyo, hueco*

hóol (hóohl) *adj.* all; *todo*

hoykeep (HOHY-keehp) *n.* lazy man; *hombre flojo*

ho' (HOH') *n.* five; *cinco*

ho' k'áal (HOH' k'áahl) (hypothetical) *n.* one hundred; *cien, ciento*

ho' lahun (HOH' LAH-hoon) (hypothetical) *n.* fifteen; *quince*

ho'ol (hoh'-ohl) *n.* head; hair; *cabeza; pelo*

ho'olheyak (HOH'-ohl-HEH-yahk) *n.* yesterday; *ayer*

ho'osik (HOH'-OHS-eek) *tr. v.* take out; extract; *sacarlo*

htaman (ah-TAH-mahn) *n.* goat, kid; sheep; *chivo, cabro; borrego*

htoot (ah-TOOHT) *n.* mute person; *persona muda*

htzo' (ah-tzoh') *n.* turkey (male); *pavo (macho)*

htz'aak (ah-TZ'AAHK) *n.* male doctor, physician; *doctor, médico*

ht'uup (ah-T'OOOP) *n.* brother (youngest); *hermano menor*

huchi (HOOCH-ee) *imper.* scram! (to pigs, chickens, etc.); *¡vete! (a puercos, pollos, etc.)*

huch' (hooch') *n.* corn dough; *maíz molido*

huch'bil (HOOCH'-beel) *adj.* ground; *molido*

huch'ik (HOOCH'-eek) *tr. v.* grind; *molerlo*

huch' k'u'um (HOOCH' k'oo'-oom) *tr. v.* grind (lime-soaked corn); *moler nixtamal/masa*

huhum p'íitil (HOO-hoom P'ÉEET-eel) *adv.* little by little; *poco a poco*

hum cháak (HOOM cháahk) *n.* thunder; *trueno*

hum puli' (hoom POO-lee') *adv.* completely, totally; *completamente, totalmente*

hump'éel (hoom P'ÉEHL) *adj., pron.* a (thing), one (thing); *un(a) (cosa)*

hump'íit (HOOM p'éeet) *n.* bit (a), little (a); *un poco, pocos*

hun (hoon) *adj., n.* single; one; *solito, solo; uno*

hun bak (HOON bahk) (hypothetical) *n.* four hundred; *cuatrocientos*

hunkúul (hoon-KÓOOL) *adj., pron.* a (tree), one (tree); *un(a) (árbol)*

hun k'áal (HOON k'áahl) (hypothetical) *n.* twenty; *veinte*

hun pik (hoon PEEK) (hypothetical) *n.* eight thousand; *ocho mil*

huntúul (hoon-TÓOOL) *adj., pron.* a (person or animal), one (person or animal); *un(a) (persona o animal)*

huntz'íit (hoon-TZ'ÉEET) *adj., pron.* a (long thing), one (long thing); *un(a) (cosa larga)*

huuh (hoooh) *n.* iguana; lizard; *iguana; lagartija*

huum (hooom) *n.* noise, sound; *ruido, sonido*

hu' chabale' (hoo' CHAHB-ahl-eh') *aux. v.* may;
se puede, se permite

hu' u biita'ale' (hooh' oo BEEE-tah'-AHL-eh') *adj.*
possible (it is); *es posible*

hu'un (hoo'-oon) *n.* book; letter; paper; *libro; carta;
papel*

hwaach (ah-WAAHCH) *n.* Mexican (male); *mexicáno*

hwáay (ah-wáahy) *n.* wizard; *brujo*

I

ich (eech) *n.* eye; face; *ojo; cara*

ichil (EECH-eel) *prep.* in, inside, within; *dentro*

ichkíil (EECH-kéeel) *in. v.* bathe; *bañarse*

iib (eeeb) *n.* bean (lima); *frijol de lima*

iícham (ÉEECH-ahm) *n.* husband; *marido, esposo*

iích'ak (ÉEE-ch'ahk) *n.* fingernail, claw; *uña*

iik (eeek) *n.* chile, pepper; *chile, ají*

iik' (eeek') *n.* air, wind; *aire, viento*

iim (eeem) *n.* bosom, breast, teat; *seno, pecho, teta*

iipil (EEEP-eel) *n.* dress (native woman's); *huipil*

iis (eees) *n.* yam, sweet potato; *camote*

iit (eeet) *n.* anus; bottom, base; *ano; base*

iitz (eeetz) *n.* sap, resin; rust; *resina o leche de árbol;
oxidado*

íitz'in (ÉEETZ'-een) *n.* brother (younger), sister
(younger); *hermano/a menor*

ileh (EEL-eh) *imper.* see it!; *¡vélo!*

ilik (EEL-eek) *tr. v.* see; *verlo*

ixbal (EESH-bahl) *in. v.* break out in a rash; *tener
roncha*

i'inah (EE'-EE-nah) *n.* seed corn; *semilla para
sembrar maíz*

K

kaab (kaahb) *n.* bee; honey; earth; world; *abeja; miel;
tierra; mundo*

kaabal (KAAHB-ahl) *adv.* below; low; *abajo; bajo*

kaacha'al (kaah-CHAH'-ahl) *adj.* broken, busted; split; fractured; *quebrado; hendido; fracturado*

kaah (kaah) *n.* place; town; *lugar; pueblo, poblacíon*

káahsik (KÁAH-seek) *tr. v.* begin; *comenzarlo*

kaahtal (KAAH-tahl) *n.* place; ranch; *lugar; rancho*

kaahtal (KAAH-tahl) *in. v.* live, reside; *vivir*

kaal (kaahl) *n.* neck; throat; voice; *cuello; garganta; voz*

káaltal (KÁAHL-tahl) *in. v.* become drunk; *emborracharse*

kaan (kaahn) *n.* snake; worm; *culebra; gusano*

kaanilha' (kaahn-eel-HAH') *n.* eel; *anguila*

káapeh (KÁAH-peh) *n.* coffee; *café*

kaax (kaahsh) *n.* chicken; *pollo*

kachik (KAH-cheek) *tr. v.* to break, split, fracture (long things); *quebrar, hender, fracturar (cosas largas)*

kala'an (KAH-lah'-ahn) *adj.* drunk, intoxicated; *borracho*

kaldo kaax (KAHL-doh KAAHSH) *n.* consumé (chicken); Sp. + Maya; *caldo de pollo*

kamp'éel (kahm-P'ÉEHL) *adj., pron.* four (inanimate things); *cuatro (cosas)*

kan (kahn) *n.* four; *cuatro*

kanantik (KAHN-ahn-teek) *tr. v.* care for (take care of); *cuidarlo*

kanik (KAHN-eek) *tr. v.* learn; *aprenderlo*

kan k'áal (KAHN k'áahl) (hypothetical) *n.* eighty; *ochenta*

kan lahun (kahn LAH-hoon) (hypothetical) *n.* fourteen; *catorce*

kantúul (kahn-TÓOOL) *adj., pron.* four (people or animals, animate things); *cuatro (personas o animales)*

kaxtik (KAHSH-teek) *tr. v.* find; look for, seek; *hallarlo, buscarlo*

kay (kahy) *n.* fish; *pescado*

ka'abeh (KAH'-AHB-eh) *n.* day after tomorrow; *la mañana siguiente*

ka'ach (kah'-ahch) *adv.* earlier, previously; *antiguamente, entonces*

ka'ah (kah'-ah) *adv.* again; *otra vez, de nuevo*

ka'ah (kah'-ah) *conj.* and; that; when; *y; que; cuando*

ka'ah (kah'-ah) *n.* metate, saddle quern, grinding stone; two; *metate; dos*

ka'aka't(e') (KAH'-AH-kah'-t[e']) *adv.* afterward; later; soon; *al rato; un poco después; más tarde*

ka'an (kah'-ahn) *n.* heaven; sky; *cielo*

ka'anal (KAH'-AHN-ahl) *adj.* up; above; high; *arriba; alto*

ka'anal (KAH'-AHN-ahl) *adv.* up; above; *arriba*

ka'anal (KAH'-AHN-ahl) *prep.* up; above; *arriba*

ka'anal (KAH'-AHN-ahl) *in. v.* tire; *cansarse*

ka'ana'an (KAH'-AH-nah'-ahn) *adj.* tired; *cansado*

ka'anche' (KAH'-AHN-che') *n.* altar; raised seedbed; *altar; plantío elevado*

ka'ansah (KAH'-AHN-sah) *n.* teacher; *maestro*

ka'ansik (KAH'-AHN-seek) *tr. v.* teach; *enseñarlo*

ka'apúul (KAH'-AH-póool) *adv.* two times, twice; *dos veces*

ka'ap'éel (KAH'-AH-p'éehl) *adj., pron.* two (inanimate things); *dos (cosas)*

ka'atúul (KAH'-AH-tóool) *adj., pron.* two (people or animals, animate things); *dos (personas o animales)*

ka' bak (KAH' bahk) (hypothetical) *n.* eight hundred; *ochocientos*

ka' k'áal (KAH' k'áahl) (hypothetical) *n.* forty; *cuarenta*

kechtik (KEHCH-teek) *tr. v.* deceive, fool, trick; *embaucarlo*

kéeh (kéeh) *n.* deer; venison; *venado; carne de venado*

keléembal (KEH-léehm-bahl) *n.* shoulder; *hombro*

kensa bixi (kehn-sah BEE-shee) *adv.* who knows; *quien sabe*

ketik (KEH-teek) *tr. v.* start (a fight); accept (a proposition); *comenzar (una pelea); aceptar (una proposicíon)*

kex (kehsh) *conj.* although; *aunque*

ke'el (keh'-ehl) *adj.* cold (meteorological); *frío*

kib (keeb) *n.* candle; *candela, vela*

kih (kee) *n.* agave; hemp; *maguey; henequin*

kiik (keeek) *n.* older sister; *hermana mayor*

kíimil (KÉEE-meel) *in. v.* die; *morir*

kiiritz' (KEEER-eetz') *in. v.* grime (around collar); *mugre*

kiis (keees) *n.* flatulence; *pedo*

kiis (keees) *in. v.* break wind; *echar pedos*

kimen (KEE-mehn) *adj.* dead; *muerto*

kinbesik (keen-BEH-seek) *tr. v.* hurt; *herirlo*

kinpahal (keen-PAH-hahl) *in. v.* hurt (oneself); *herirse*

kinsik (KEEN-seek) *tr. v.* kill; *matarlo*

kisin (KEES-een) *n.* devil; *diablo*

kitam (KEE-tahm) *n.* boar; collared peccary (*Pecari tajacu*); *jabalí; coche del monte*

ki' (kee') *adj.* tasty; *sabroso*

ki'ichpam (KEE'-EECH-pahm) *adj.* good-looking, pretty; *hermoso, guapo, bonito*

ki'imak óol (KEE'-EE-mahk ÓOHL) *adj.* content, happy; *contento*

koh (koh) *n.* beak; tooth; puma; *pico; diente; puma*

konik (KOHN-eek) *tr. v.* sell; *venderlo*

kóoch (kóohch) *adj.* broad, wide; *ancho*

kóok (kóohk) *adj.* deaf; *sordo*

kool (koohl) *n.* personal cornfield (milpa); *milpa*

kóolik (KÓOHL-eek) *tr. v.* pull; *jalarlo*

koolnáal (KOOHL-náahl) *n.* farmer, milpa tiller; *campesino, milpero*

kóom (kóohm) *adj.* narrow; short; *estrecho; corto*

koonol (KOOHN-ohl) *n.* vendor (male), salesman; *vendedor*

koos (koohs) *n.* falcon; *halcón*

kopik (KOH-peek) *tr. v.* coil (rope), roll, twist, screw; *enrollar soga*

ko'oh (koh'-oh) *adj.* expensive; *caro*

ko'olel (KOH'-ohl-EHL) *n.* woman; *mujer*

ko'oten (KOH'-OH-tehn) *imper.* come!; *¡ven!*

ko'ox (koh'-osh) *imper.* let's go!; *¡vámanos! (vamos)*

kuchik (KOOCH-eek) *tr. v.* carry (on the back); *cargarlo (en la espalda), llevarlo*

kula'an (koo-LAH'-ahn) *adj.* seated; *sentado*

kultal (KOOL-tahl) *in. v.* sit down; *sentarse*

ku páahtal (koo PÁAH-tahl) *in. v.* can (able to); *se puede*

kuuch (koooch) *n.* burden, load; obligation; *carga; obligación*

kúuk (kóook) *n.* elbow; *codo*

kuutz (koootz) *n.* wild oscelated turkey (*Agriocharis ocellata*); *pavo del monte*

kuxa'an (KOO-shah'-ahn) *adj.* alive, living; *vivo*

kuxtal (KOOSH-tahl) *n.* life; *vida*

ku'uk (KOO'-ook) *n.* squirrel; *ardilla*

K'

k'aab/k'aa' (k'aahb/k'aah') *n.* broth; juice; *caldo; jugo*

k'aaba' (K'AAHB-ah') *n.* name; *nombre*

k'aab china (k'aahb CHEE-nah) *n.* orange juice; *jugo de naranja*

k'áah (k'áah) *adj.* bitter; *amargo*

k'áak' (k'áahk') *n.* fire; *fuego*

k'aalal (K'AAHL-ahl) *adj.* closed, locked; *cerrado*

k'áan (k'áahn) *n.* hammock; *hamaca*

k'áanche' (K'ÁAHN-cheh') *n.* stool; *banqueta para sentarse*

k'aas (k'aahs) *adj.* bad; *malo*

k'aas (k'aahs) *n.* evil; *mal, maldad*

k'aas wayak' (k'aahs WAHY-ahk') *n.* nightmare; *mal sueño, pesadilla*

k'áat (k'áaht) *in. v.* (I) want; *quiero*

k'aatal (K'AAH-tahl) *adj.* crossed; *cruzado*

k'áatik (K'ÁAHT-eek) *tr. v.* ask for; *pedirlo, preguntarlo*

k'áax (k'áahsh) *adj.* angry; hateful; *enojado; odioso*

k'áax (k'áahsh) *n.* brush, weed, forest, jungle; *monte, bosque*

k'aay (k'aahy) *n.* music, song; *canción*

k'aay (k'aahy) *in. v.* sing; *cantar*

k'ab (k'ahb) *n.* arm; hand; branch; *brazo; mano; rama*

k'abéet (K'AHB-éet) *adj.* necessary; *necesario*

k'ahóol (K'AH-óohl) *tr. v.* know (someone); *conocerlo*

k'ahóoltik (K'AH-óohl-TEEK) *tr. v.* recognize; *reconocerlo*

k'alik (K'AHL-eek) *tr. v.* close; *cerrarlo*

k'amik (K'AHM-eek) *tr. v.* receive; *recibir*

k'an (k'ahn) *adj.* ripe; yellow; *maduro; amarillo*

k'as (k'ahs) *n.* somewhat; *de una parte, un poquito*

k'as ke'el (K'AHS keh'-ehl) *adj.* cool; *medio frío*

k'as k'íilkab (k'ahs K'ÉEEL-kahb) *adj.* muggy; *medio sudando, húmedo*

k'at (k'aht) *n.* clay; *barro*

k'axab nak' (K'AHSH-ahb nahk') *n.* belt, strap; *cinturón, faja*

k'axik (K'AHSH-eek) *tr. v.* tie; *amarrarlo*

k'a'am (K'AH'-ahm) *adj.* harsh; strong; *recio; fuerte*

k'a'ana'an (K'AH'-AH-nah'-ahn) *adj.* important, necessary; *importante, necesario*

k'a'atik (K'AH'-AH-teek) *tr. v.* grill, roast; *asarlo*

k'a'bil (K'AH'-beel) *adj.* grilled, roasted; *asado*

k'a'bil bak' (K'AH'-beel BAHK') *adj.* grilled (meat); (*carne*) *asada*

k'eban (K'EH-bahn) *adj.* wrong, sin; *pecado*

k'éek'en (K'ÉEH-k'ehn) *n.* pig; *puerco*

k'éewel (K'ÉEH-wehl) *n.* hide, leather, skin; *piel, pellejo, cuero*

k'eexel (K'EEHSH-ehl) *adj.* changed, exchanged, substituted; *cambiado, trocado*

k'exik (K'EHSH-eek) *tr. v.* change; exchange; substitute; *cambiarlo, trocarlo*

k'eyem (K'EH-yehm) *n.* gruel, posol; *pozole*

k'eyik (K'EHY-eek) *tr. v.* reprimand, scold; *reprenderlo, reñirlo*

k'íilkab (K'ÉEEL-kahb) *adj.* hot (weather), humid (weather); perspiration; (*hace*) *calor, húmedo; sudor*

k'iin (k'eeen) *n.* day; sun; time; *día; sol; tiempo*

k'íinal (K'ÉEE-nahl) *adj.* heated up; hot; lukewarm; tepid; *calientado; tibio*

k'inan (in) ho'ol' (K'EEN-ahn een HOH'-OHL') *n. phr.* headache; *dolor de cabeza*

k'iwi' (K'EE-wee') *n.* annatto (red food dye); *achiote*

k'i'ik' (k'ee'-eek') *n.* blood; *sangre*

k'i'inam (K'EE'-EE-nahm) *n.* pain; *dolor*

k'i'ix (K'EE'-eesh) *n.* thorn; *espina*

k'i'ix pech ooch (K'EE'-EESH pehch OOHCH) *n.* porcupine; *cuerpo espín*

k'oha'an (K'OH-hah'-ahn) *adj.* sick; *enfermo*

k'oha'anil (k'oh-HAH'-AHN-eel) *n.* illness; *enfermedad*

k'oha'antal (k'oh-HAH'-AHN-tahl) *in. v.* ill (to become); *enfermarse*

k'o no'och (K'OH noh'-ohch) *n.* chin (literally "double chin"); *barbilla*

k'ooben (K'OOH-behn) *n.* hearth; kitchen; *fogón; cocina*

k'óol (k'óohl) *n.* broth; stew; *caldo; guiso*

k'osik (K'OHS-eek) *tr. v.* cut with scissors; *cortarlo con tijera*

k'oxol (K'OHSH-ohl) *n.* mosquito; *mosquito, mosco*

k'o'ox (K'OH'-ohsh) *adj.* wild; *bravo, salvaje, cimarrón*

k'ubik (K'OOB-eek) *tr. v.* deliver; *entregarlo*

k'ubul (K'OOB-ool) *n.* oriole; *oriol*

k'uchul (K'OOCH-ool) *in. v.* arrive; *llegar*

k'uho'ob (K'OO-hoh'-ohb) *pl. n.* gods, saints; *dioses, santos*

k'ulu' (K'OOL-oo') *n.* raccoon; *mapache*
k'úum (k'óoom) *n.* pumpkin, squash; *calabaza*
k'uutz (k'oootz) *n.* marijuana; tobacco; *marijuana; tabaco*
k'uxu' (K'OO-shoo') *n.* annatto (red food dye); *achiote*
k'u' (k'oo') *n.* nest; *nido*
k'u'uk'um (k'oo'-ook'-OOM) *n.* feathers; *plumas*

L

láah (láah) *adj.* all; *todo*
láak' (láahk') *adj.* other; *otro*
láak' (láahk') *n.* parent; relative; spouse; *pariente, miembro de familia; esposo*
láak'tzil (LÁAHK'-tzeel) *n.* true sibling; *hermano(a) verdadero(a)*
láal (láahl) *n.* nettle; *ortiga, chichicasta*
láayli'(e') (láahy-LEE'-[eh']) *adv.* always; *siempre*
lahka'a (LAH-kah'-ah) (hypothetical) *n.* twelve; *doce*
lahun (LAH-hoon) (hypothetical) *n.* ten; *diez*
lahun k'áal (LAH-hoon K'ÁAHL) (hypothetical) *n.* two hundred; *doscientos*
lak'in (LAH-k'een) *n.* east; *este, oriente*
le beetik (leh BEEEH-teek) *adv.* therefore; *por eso*
le ka'a p'éelil (leh kah'-ah P'ÉEEH-leel) *adj., prep.* possibly; *posible*
lela' (LEH-lah') *pron.* this (one); *éste, ésta*
lelo' (LEH-loh') *pron.* that (one); *ése, ésa*
le' (leh') *n.* leaf; *hoja*
líik'il (LÉEEK'-eel) *in. v.* arise, rise; *levantarse*
li'isik (LEE'-EES-eek) *tr. v.* raise; *levantarlo*
li'isik u ba (LEE'-EES-eek oo BAH) *refl. v.* ready (oneself); *prepararse*
li'sik (LEE'-seek) *tr. v.* make ready, prepare; *alistarlo, prepararlo*
loob (loohb) *n.* accident, misfortune; injury, wound; *accidente, infortunio; daño, herrida*
lóob (lóohb) *n.* digging stick; *coa*
loobil (LOOHB-eel) *n.* wound; blow; *herida; golpe*
lool (loohl) *n.* flower, rose; *flor, rosa*
loxik (LOHSH-eek) *tr. v.* punch (with fist); *pegarlo con puño cerado*
lúubul (LÓOOB-ool) *in. v.* fall; *caerse*

luuch (loooch) *n.* gourd (from a tree); *jícara, calabaza de árbol*

lukum (LOOK-oom) *adj.* fine, nice, delicate; *fino, bueno, delicado*

luk'ul (LOOK'-ool) *in. v.* leave; *quitarse*

luuk' (loook') *in. v.* swallow; *tragar*

lúub (lóoob) *n.* league (measure); *legua*

lu' (loo') *n.* catfish; *bagre*

lu'um (loo'-oom) *n.* dirt, earth, soil; *suelo, tierra*

M

máak (máahk) *n.* man, person; *hombre, persona*

máakalmáak (MÁAHK-ahl-MÁAHK) *inter.* which?; *¿cuál?*

máakan (MÁAH-kahn) *n.* arbor, bower; *enramada*

maam (maahm) *n.* mother; *madre*

máan (máahn) *in. v.* pass by; *pasar*

máasewáal (máah-SEH-wáahl) *n.* Indian, inferior; *indígena, mazehual, inferior*

máaskab (MÁAHS-kahb) *n.* iron; machete; *hierro; machete*

máaskabil xamach (máahs-KAHB-eel SHAH-mahch) *n.* griddle (iron); *comal de hierro*

máax (máahsh) *pron.* who; *quien*

máaxi' (máahsh-EE') *inter.* who?; *¿quién?*

machik (MAHCH-eek) *tr. v.* grab, grasp; *agarrarlo*

mach' (mahch') *tr. v.* flatten (something); *allanar, aplanar, aplastar*

maháantik (MAH-háahn-teek) *tr. v.* lend, loan; *prestarlo*

mahan (MAH-hahn) *adj.* borrowed; *prestado*

mahan yuum (MAH-hahn YOOOM) *n.* stepfather (borrowed father); *padrastro*

mak'antik (MAH-k'ahn-TEEK) *tr. v.* make (by hand); prepare; *hacerlo a mano; prepararlo*

maldisyontik (MAHL-dees-yohn-TEEK) *tr. v.* curse; (Sp. + Maya) *maldecirlo*

manik (MAHN-eek) *tr. v.* buy; *comprarlo*

mansik (MAHN-seek) *tr. v.* pass; *pasarlo*

ma' (mah') *adv.* no, not; *no*

ma'a kaal (MAH'-AH kaahl) *adj.* hoarse; *ronco*

ma'alob (mah'-AHL-ohb) *adj.* good, OK, well; *bien, bueno, adecuado*

ma'a taan (MAH'-AH taahn) *adv.* won't; *no*

ma'a tech (MAH'-AH tehch) *adv.* never; *jamás*

ma'ax (mah'-ahsh) *n.* monkey; *mono*

ma' ko'ohi' (MAH' koh'-oh-hee') *adj.* cheap; *barato*

ma' teeni' (mah' TEEHN-ee') *adv.* not me; *yo no*

ma' tu páahtal (mah' too PÁAH-tahl) *in. v.* cannot; *no se puede*

ma' u cha'bal (mah' oo CHAH'-bahl) *aux. v.* may not; *no se permite*

ma' ya'abi' (MAH' yah'-ah-bee') *adj.* little, not much; *no mucho, poco*

méek'ik (MÉEH-k'-eek) *tr. v.* embrace; *abrazarlo*

meerech (MEEHR-ehch) *n.* lizard (species of); *lagartija (una especie)*

mehen (MEH-hehn) *adj.* little, small; *pequeño, chico*

mentik (MEHN-teek) *tr. v.* make; *hacerlo*

meyah (MEH-yah) *n.* work; *trabajo*

meyah (MEH-yah) *in. v.* work; *trabajar*

me'ex (meh'-ehsh) *n.* beard, moustache; *barba, bigote*

miis (meees) *n.* cat; *gato*

míis (méees) *n.* broom; *escoba*

míistik (MÉEES-teek) *tr. v.* sweep; *barrerlo*

mina'an (MEE-nah'-ahn) *adv.* there isn't/there aren't; *no hay*

mix ba'al (meesh BAH'-ahl) *pron.* nothing; *nada*

mix bik'in (meesh BEE-k'een) *adv.* never; *nunca*

mix máak (MEESH máahk) *pron.* no one; *ninguno, nadie*

mix táan u beeta'ale' (meesh TÁAHN oo beeh-tah'-AHL-eh) *adj.* not possible; *no es posible*

mix tu'ux (MEESH too'-oosh) *n.* nowhere; *en ninguna parte*

mootz (moohtz) *n.* root; *raíz*

mo' (moh') *n.* macaw; *guacamayo*

mukik (MOOK-eek) *tr. v.* bury; *enterrarlo, sepultarlo*

mu(n)yal (MOO[N]-yahl) *n.* cloud; *nube*

mut (moot) *n.* bird; *ave, pájaro*

muuch (moooch) *n.* frog, toad; *rana, sapo*

muuk' (moook') *adj.* forceful; *fuerte*

muuk' (moook') *n.* strength; *fuerza*

muul (moool) *n.* hill; pyramid; *cerro; pirámide*

muxbil (MOOSH-beel) *adj.* ground (into meal); *molido*

N

náach (náahch) *adj.* distant; *lejos*

náachil (NÁAHCH-eel) *n.* distance; *distancia*

naapul (NAAH-pool) *adv.* direct, directly; *directo, inmediato*

naapulak (naah-POOL-ahk) *adv.* immediately, right away; *en seguido*

naatz' (naahtz') *adj.* near; *cerca*

naatz'al (NAAHTZ'-ahl) *in. v.* approach; *acercar*

naatz'ik (NAAHTZ'-eek) *tr. v.* approach; *acercarlo*

náay (náahy) *in. v.* dream; *soñar*

nah (nah) *n.* house; *casa*

nahil (NAH-eel) *n.* building, home; *edificio, casa*

nah' (nah') *n.* mother; *madre*

nak' (nahk') *n.* abdomen, stomach, belly; *barriga, panza, estómago*

nak' (nahk') *tr. v.* abandon; *abandonar*

nal (nahl) *n.* corn (ear of); *elote*

naptzah (NAHP-tzah) *tr. v.* become accustomed to; *acostumbrarlo, habituarlo*

na'akal (NAH'-AHK-ahl) *tr. v.* climb; *subir*

na'atik (NAH'-AH-teek) *tr. v.* understand; *entenderlo, comprenderlo*

néen (néehn) *n.* mirror; *espejo*

neek' (neehk') *n.* seed; *semilla, pepita*

neh (neh) *n.* tail; *cola, rabo*

níix (néeesh) *n.* incline, slope; *cuesta, ladera, inclinación*

niixil (NEEESH-eel) *adj.* tilted; *inclinado*

nikte' (NEEK-teh') *n.* flower, frangipani; *flor, frangipaniero*

nixik (NEESH-eek) *tr. v.* tilt; *inclinarlo*

ni' (nee') *n.* nose; *nariz*

nohoch (NOH-hohch) *adj.* big, large; old; *gran, grande; viejo*

nohochil (noh-hoh-CHEEL) *n.* size; *tamaño*

nohoch ko'olel (NOH-hoch koh'-ohl-EHL) *n.* old woman; *vieja*

nohoch taat(ah) (NOH-hohch TAAHT-[ah]) *n.* grandfather; *abuelo*

nohoch wíinik (NOH-hoch WÉEEN-eek) *n.* old man; *viejo*

nohol (NOH-hohl) *n.* south; *sur*

nok'ol (NOHK'-ohl) *n.* worm; *gusano*

noohoch(il) (NOOH-hohch-[EEL]) *n.* boss; *jefe*

nóokoy (NÓOHK-ohy) *adj.* cloudy, overcast; *nublado*

nóokoytal (NÓOHK-ohy-tahl) *in. v.* overcast (to become); *nublarse*

nook' (noohk') *n.* clothes, clothing; dress; *ropa; falda*

no'oh (noh'-oh) *n.* right side; *lado derecho*

nukuch (NOO-kooch) *adj.* large (pl.), big (pl.); *grandes*

nuukbesah (noook-BEH-sah) *tr. v.* adjust; *ajustar, arreglar, componer*

núukik (NÓOOK-eek) *tr. v.* answer; *contestarlo, responderlo*

nuuktak (NOOK-tahk) *adj.* big; *grande*

nuum (nooom) *adj.* ignorant, stupid; lazy; *estúpido; perezoso*

nuxiib (NOO-sheeeb) *adj.* old man; *hombre viejo, anciano*

nu'ukul (NOO'-OOK-ool) *n.* reason; explanation; utensil, tool; *razón; explicación; instrumento, herramiento, utensilio*

O

och kaan (OHCH kaahn) *n.* boa constrictor; *culebra tipo de boa*

ohéeltik (oh-HÉEHL-teek) *tr. v.* understand, notice, know; *reconocerlo, notar*

oka'an k'iin (oh-KAH'-AHN k'eeen) *n.* evening; *tarde*

oklik (OHK-leek) *tr. v.* steal; *hurtarlo, robarlo*

okol (OHK-ohl) *in. v.* enter; *entrar*

okom (OHK-ohm) *n.* pillar, post; *pilar, horcón, poste*

oksik (OK-seek) *tr. v.* introduce, insert; *introducirlo, meterlo*

ok'ol (OHK'-ohl) *in. v.* cry, weep; *llorar*

ok'ot (OH-k'oht) *in. v.* dance; *bailar*

ooch (oohch) *n.* fox; weasel; *zorro; comadreja*

oohel (OOH-hehl) *tr. v.* know; *saberlo, conocerlo*

ook (oohk) *n.* foot; *pie*

ookol (OOHK-ohl) *in. v.* steal; *hurtar, robar*

ookolbil (OOHK-ohl-BEEL) *adj.* stolen; *robado, hurtado*

óok'ot (ÓOH-k'oht) *n.* dance; *baile*

óol (óohl) *n.* heart; will; energy; spirit; *corazón; ganas; energía; espíritu*

oon (oohn) *n.* avocado; *aguacate*

óop (óohp) *n.* soursop (custard apple); *anona*

oop' (oohp') *n.* toast; *tostada*

óotzil (ÓOHTZ-eel) *adj.* poor; *pobre*

óox (óohsh) *n.* three; *tres*

óox k'áal (ÓOHSH k'aahl) (hypothetical) *n.* sixty; *sesenta*

óox lahun (óohsh LAH-hoon) (hypothetical) *n.* thirteen; *trece*

óoxpúul (ÓOHSH-póool) *adv.* three times; *tres veces*

óoxp'éel (ÓOHSH-p'éehl) *adj., pron.* three (inanimate things); *tres (cosas)*

óoxtúul (ÓOHSH-tóool) *adj., pron.* three (people or animals, animate things); *tres (personas o animales)*

otoch (oh-tohch) *n.* home; *hogar*

oxo'ontik (OHSH-oh'-ohn-TEEK) *tr. v.* shell corn; *desgranarlo*

o'och (OH'-ohch) *n.* tortilla, food; *tortilla, comida*

P

paach (paahch) *n.* back; *espalda, lomo*

páahtal (PÁAH-tahl) *adj.* be able to; *poder*

páak (páahk) *in. v.* clear, weed; *chapear, desherbar*

páaktik (PÁAHK-teek) *tr. v.* cut brush, weed; *chapearlo, desherbarlo*

páak'am (PÁAHK'-ahm) *n.* cactus (prickly pear); *nopal, tuna*

paal (paahl); *n.* infant, child, minor; son; *niño(a), menor; hijo*

páanik (PÁAHN-eek) *tr. v.* dig, scrape; *cavarlo*

páap (páahp) *adj.* hot, spicy; *picante*

paapah (PAAH-pah) *n.* father; Sp. loanword; *papá, padre*

paapil (PAAHP-eel) *adj.* biting; sharp; *picante*

páatal (PÁAHT-ahl) *adj.* be able (to be able to); *poder*

páayooch (PÁAHY-oohch) *n.* skunk; *zorillo*

páaytik (PÁAHY-teek) *tr. v.* pull; *jalarlo*

pah (pah) *adj.* acidic, sour; *ácido, ágrio*

pakteh (PAHK-teh) *imper.* look at it!; *¡mírelo!*

paktik (PAHK-teek) *tr. v.* look (at); *mirarlo*

pak' (pahk') *n.* masonry, wall (of masonry);
mampostería

pak'áal (PAHK'-áahl) *n.* citrus fruit, sour orange tree;
cítricos, naranja agria; naranjo agrio

pak'ach (PAHK'-ahch) *in. v.* make tortillas; *tortear*

pak'achtik (PAHK'-ahch-teek) *tr. v.* make tortillas,
pound; *tortearlo, machacarlo*

pak'al (PAHK'-ahl) *n.* plant; *planta*

pak'al (PAHK'-ahl) *in. v.* sow, plant; *sembrar*

pak'a'an (PAHK'-ah'-ahn) *par.* sown; *sembrado*

pak'ik (PAHK'-eek) *tr. v.* sow, plant; *sembrarlo*

pak'il nah (pahk'-eel NAH) *n.* stone house; *casa
de piedra*

payik (PAHY-eek) *tr. v.* call; *llamar*

payk'ab (PAHY-k'ahb) *in. v.* wave, signal (by hand);
señalar, señal

pay wakax (pahy WAHK-ahsh) *n.* bullfight; *torear,
corrida de toros*

pa'at (pah'-aht) *in. v.* wait; *esperar*

pa'atik (PAH'-AHT-eek) *tr. v.* expect, wait for; *esperarlo*

pa'ik (PAH'-eek) *tr. v.* break; *romperlo, quebrarlo*

pechéech (PEH-chéehch) *n.* spindle; winch; *malacate;
huso*

peech (peehch) *n.* tick (insect); *garrapata*

péek (péehk) *n.* movement; *movimiento*

péek (péehk) *in. v.* move; throb; wiggle; *moverse;
palpitarse; menearse*

péeksik (PÉEHK-seek) *tr. v.* move, shake; *moverlo,
sacudirlo*

peek' (peehk') *n.* dog; *perro*

péepem (PÉEHP-ehm) *n.* butterfly; *mariposa*

peetz' (peehtz') *n.* snare, trap; *trampa*

pek'a'an (PEH-K'AH'-ahn) *adj.* flat; lying (on the
ground); *llano; tirado/hechado en el suelo*

petz'ik (PEHTZ'-eek) *tr. v.* crush, smash; detain;
apretar, destrozar; detener

pibil kaax (PEEB-eel kaahsh) *n.* chicken (baked);
pollo pibil

pibil k'éek'en (PEEB-eel k'éeh-k'ehn) *n.* pork (baked,
roasted); *conchinita pibil*

pichi' (PEECH-ee') *n.* guava; *guayaba*

pich' (peech') *n.* thrush (bird); *tordo (cantor),
zorzal (ave)*

píib (péeeb) *n.* cooking pit (bar-b-que pit); *barbacoa, horno, pib*

píim (péeem) *adj.* thick; *grueso, gordo*

piitoh (PEEE-toh) *n.* flute, whistle; Sp. loanword; *pito, flauta*

piitor(l)eeyaal (PEEE-to-r[l]eeh-yaahl) *n.* toucan; Sp. loanword; *pitoreal*

piitz' (peeetz') *n.* cotton (combed); *algodón desmotado*

píix (péeesh) *n.* case; cover; knee; *caja, tapa, vaina; rodilla*

pik (peek) *n.* bedbug; *chinche*

pitik (PEE-teek) *tr. v.* disrobe; scoop up excrement; *desnudarse, quitar la ropa; sacar excremento con cuchara*

pixaan (PEESH-aahn) *n.* soul, spirit; *alma, espíritu*

pokbil (POHK-beel) *adj.* roasted; toasted; *asado; tostado*

pok chuk (POHK chook) *n.* grilled (meat); *asado (carne)*

polok (POHL-ohk) *adj.* fat, thick; *gordo, grueso*

pool (poohl) *n.* head; *cabeza*

poolkil (POOHL-keel) *n.* thickness; *gordura*

poos (poohs) *adj.* faded, pale, palid; hollow; *descolorido, palido, desteñido; waco*

popoxkan (poh-pohsh-KAHN) *n.* ant (biting); *hormiga que muerde*

potik (POHT-eek) *tr. v.* pass through, penetrate; *transpasarlo, penetrarlo*

puch'ik (POOCH'-eek) *in. v.* mash, crush, bruise; *magullar, despachurrar, moler*

puh (poo) *n.* pus; *pus, materia de llaga*

puksi'ik'al (POOK-see'-eek'-ahl) *n.* heart; *corazón*

puuk (poook) *adj.* cloudy (liquid); muddy; *turbio*

puuk' (poook') *adj.* scrambled; *revueltos*

puul (poool) *adv.* all at once; *todo una vez*

puut (pooot) *n.* papaya; *papaya*

púutz' (póootz') *n.* needle; *aguja*

púutz'ul (PÓOOTZ'-ool) *in. v.* escape, get away; *escaparse*

P'

p'aak (p'aahk) *n.* tomato; *jitomate, tomate*

p'áatal (P'ÁAH-tahl) *in. v.* remain, stay; *quedarse*

p'atik (P'AHT-eek) *tr. v.* leave; *dejarlo*

p'eeka'an (p'eeh-KAH'-AHN) *par.* hated (with agent); *aborrecido, abominado*

p'ektik (P'EHK-teek) *tr. v.* hate, dislike, detest; *odiarlo*

p'isik (P'EES-eek) *tr. v.* measure, weigh; *medirlo, pesarlo*

p'isik'an (P'EES-eek'-ahn) *n.* land, mecate (unit of 20 × 20 m; unit of land); *mecate*

p'ok (p'ohk) *n.* hat; *sombrero*

p'o'a'al (P'OH'-ah'-ahl) *adj.* washed; *lavado*

p'o'ik (P'OH'-eek) *tr. v.* wash; *lavarlo*

p'uchik (P'OOCH-eek) *tr. v.* beat (with a stick), flail, thresh; *golpearlo con palo, desgranar*

p'uuch (p'oooch) *in. v.* beat, flail (grain or fruit), thresh; *batear, desgranar*

p'uuhul (P'OOO-hool) *adj.* angered, frightened, bothered; *enojado, espantado, molestado*

p'u'uhsik (P'OO'-OO-seek) *tr. v.* bother, scare; *alborotarlo, molestarlo, espantarlo*

p'u'ukil iit (P'OO'-OOK-eel EEET) *n.* buttock, rump; *nalga*

S

sáabin (SÁAH-been) *n.* weasel; *comadreja*

sáabukaan (SÁAH-boo-kaahn) *n.* bag, sack; *bolsa, morral*

saahkil (SAAHK-eel) *n.* fear; *miedo, temor*

saak' (saahk') *n.* itch/itching; *comezón*

sáak' (sáahk') *n.* cigar; locust; *cigarra; langosta de tierra, saltamontes*

sáal (sáahl) *adj.* light (weight); *ligero, no pesado*

sáam (sáam) *adv.* already; *ya, listo*

sáamal (SÁAH-mahl) *n.* tomorrow; *mañana*

saampol (SAAHM-pohl) *n.* tayra (*Tayra barbara*); *oso colmenero, perico ligero*

sáansamal (SÁAHN-sah-mahl) *adv.* daily; *diario, cada día*

sáas (sáahs); *adj.* clear; *claro*

sáasil (SÁAHS-eel) *n.* light; *luz*

sáastal (SÁAHS-tahl) *in. v.* dawn; light (to become); *amanecer*

saatal (SAAH-tahl) *adj.* lost; *perdido*

sabak (SAH-bahk) *n.* soot; *tizne*

sahahkúuns (SAH-hah-kóoons) *tr. v.* frighten, scare; *asustarlo, espantarlo*

sahkab/saskab (SAHK-ahb/SAHS-kahb) *n.* white earth (used in mortar); *roca calcárea deleznable, sascab*

sak (sahk) *adj.* white; *blanco*

sakan (SAHK-ahn) *n.* corn dough; *masa*

sak bok (SAHK bohk) *n.* heron (white); *garza blanca*

saksa' (SAHK-sah') *n.* atole (corn gruel); cornmeal beverage; *atole; atole con cáscara*

sam (sahm) *adv.* rather, slightly; *apenas, un poco*

satpahal (saht-PAH-hahl) *in. v.* disappear, get lost; *desaparecerse*

satik (SAHT-eek) *tr. v.* lose; *perderlo*

satz'ik (SAHTZ'-eek) *tr. v.* extend, stretch; *estirarlo*

sayab (SAHY-ahb) *n.* fountain, spring, source; *fuente, ojo de agua*

sayap ha' (SAHY-ahp HA') *n.* well, spring; *pozo, ojo de agua*

sa' (sah') *n.* atole (corn gruel); cornmeal beverage; *atole*

séeb (séehb) *adv.* quickly; *rápido*

séeb (séehb) *in. v.* hurry; *estar de prisa*

séebak (SÉEHB-ahk) *adj.* quick; *rápido*

séeb u meyah (SÉEHB ooh MEHY-ah) *adj.* diligent; *diligente*

séekuntik (SÉEH-koon-teek) *in. v.* hurry; *estar de prisa*

sen (sehn) *adv.* very (evaluates quantity); -*ísimo, mucho*

senbesah (sehn-BEH-sah) *tr. v.* adorn; *adornar, ornamentar*

sen ma'alob (sehn MAH'-AHL-ohb) *adj.* super, very good; *buenísimo*

sen utz (SEHN ootz) *adj.* very nice; *buenísimo, muy bien*

se'en (seh'-ehn) *n.* cold, catarrh; *catarro*

se'enik (SEH'-EHN-eek) *tr. v.* cough (dry); *toser*

síihbil (SÉEEB-eel) *n.* gift, present; *regalo*

síihik (SÉEE-heek) *tr. v.* give (as a gift); *regalarlo*

síihil (SÉEE-heel) *in. v.* born (to be); *nacer*

síim (séeem) *n.* mucus; *moco*

síina'an (séee-NAH'-AHN) *n.* scorpion; *escorpion*

síinik (SÉEEN-eek) *n.* ant; *hormiga*

siip/si'ip(il) (SEEEP/SEE'-EEP-[eel]) *n.* error, fault; sin; *error, yerro, culpa, pecado*

síis (sées) *adj.* cold, cool; *frío*

síiskuntik (SÉEES-koon-teek) *tr. v.* freeze; *enfriarlo*

siit (seeet) *n.* reed, straw; *popote*

síit' (séeet') *in. v.* bounce, jump; *saltar, brincar*

sikil (SEEK-eel) *n.* pumpkin seeds, squash seeds; *pepitas de calabaza*

si' (see') *n.* firewood; *leña*

sohol (SOH-hohl) *n.* debris (from plants), trash; *basura de hojas secas, basura*

sóol (sóohl) *n.* bark (tree); husk, shell; *corteza; carapacho, cáscara*

sootz' (soohtz') *n.* bat; *murciélago*

so'oso'ok' (SOH'-OH-soh'-ok') *adj.* tangled (in several places); bagasse (short fiber residue of henequin); *enredado; bagazo*

so'oso'ok' (SOH'-OH-soh'-ok') *n.* bagasse (short fiber residue of henequin); *bagazo*

suhuy (SOO-hooy) *adj.* intact; virgin; *intacto; virgen*

suhuy k'áax (SOO-hooy K'ÁAHSH) *n.* virgin forest; *monte virgen (nunca labrada)*

suhuy paal (SOO-hooy paahl) *n.* maiden; *muchacha*

suku'un (SOO-koo'-oon) *n.* older brother; *hermano mayor*

sup'a'an (SOO-p'ah'-ahn) *adj.* blocked (with poles); *cerrado (con palos)*

sup'ik (SOOP'-eek) *tr. v.* block (a road); close; fence in (with poles or posts); *tapar (un camino); cerrarlo; cercar con postes o palos*

sutik (SOO-teek) *tr. v.* return; *devolverlo*

suuk (soook) *adj.* tame; accustomed; *manso; acostumbrado*

súuk'in bah (SÓOO-k'een BAH) *in. v.* abstain; *abstenerse*

suum (sooom) *n.* lasso, rope; *lazo, soga*

suut (sooot) *in. v.* return; *regresar*

su'lak (SOO'-lahk) *adj.* ashamed, embarrassed; *avergüenzada*

su'tal (SOO'-tahl) *n.* dignity; *dignidad*

su'uk (soo'-ook) *n.* grass, hay; *zacate*

su'utal (SOO'-OO-tahl) *n.* embarrassment, shame; *vergüenza*

su'utal (SOO'-OO-tahl) *in. v.* be returned; thicken, become dense; *devolver; espesar*

T

taahal (TAAH-hahl) *adj.* sliced; *rabinado*
taak (taahk) *aspect marker* anxious; *ansioso*
taak (taahk) *in. v.* want; *querer, tener ganas*
taak'in (TAAH-k'een) *n.* gold; money; *oro; dinero*
taak'inal (TAAH-k'een-ahl) *adj.* rich; *rico*
taal (taahl) *in. v.* come; *venir*
taam (taahm) *adj.* deep; low; *profundo; hondo*
táaman (TÁAHM-ahn) *n.* liver; *hígado*
táan (táahn) *n.* front; *frente*
táan (táahn) *prep.* before; *delante, enfrente*
táanil (TÁAHN-eel) *prep.* in front of; *enfrente de*
taasik (TAAHS-eek) *tr. v.* bring; *traerlo*
taat(ah) (TAAHT-[ah]) *n.* father; *padre*
táax (táahsh) *adj.* flat, smooth; *llano, plano*
tah (tah) *in. v.* mature, ripen; cook (as in beans);
    madurarse, sazonarse
tahal (TAH-hahl) *in. v.* bake; boil; cook; *cocer por
    horno; hervir; cocer*
tahal (TAH-hahl) *tr. v.* bake; boil; cook; *cocerlo por
    horno; hervirlo, cocerlo*
tahik (tah-eek) *tr. v.* slice; *rabanar*
tak (tahk) *prep.* until; from; *hasta; de, desde*
tak domingo (tahk doh-MEENG-goh) *prep.* until
    Sunday; *hasta el domingo*
tak'an (TAH-k'ahn) *adj.* cooked; mature, ripe; *cocido;
    maduro*
taman (TAH-mahn) *n.* cotton; *algodón*
tamax chi' (TAH-mahsh CHEE') *n.* omen,
    prognostication; *agüero*
tanilí (tahn-eel-EE) *adv.* already; *ya, desde entonces,
    antes de ahora*
ta' (tah') *n.* excrement, droppings; *excremento, mierda*
ta'ab (tah'-ahb) *n.* salt; *sal*
ta'abik (TAH'-AHB-eek) *tr. v.* salt; *salar*
ta'akik (TAH'-AHK-eek) *tr. v.* care for (take care of),
    protect, hide, keep; *cuidarlo, esconderlo, guardarlo*
ta'an (tah'-ahn) *n.* lime (calcium carbonate,
    whitewash); *cal*
ta'aytak (TAH'-AHY-tahck) *prep.* almost, about to, on
    the verge of; *ya mero, inminente, casí*
ta'ik u bah (TAH'-eek oo bah) *refl.* humiliate oneself;
    defecate on oneself; *defecarse*

teech (teehch) *2nd p. s. pron.* you; *tú*
teen (teehn) *1st p. s. pron.* I; me; *yo; me*
ten (tehn) *prep. phr.* to me (contraction of *ti'* and *teen*);
 a mí
te' (teh') *adv.* here; *allí*
te'ela' (TEH'-EH-lah') *adv.* right here; *allí*
te'elo' (TEH'-EH-loh') *adv.* right there; *allá*
tihil (TEE-heel) *in. v.* dry; *secarse*
tihsik (TEE-seek) *tr. v.* dry; *secarlo*
tíit (téeet) *in. v.* shake; *sacudirse*
tíitik (TÉEET-eek) *tr. v.* shake; *sacudirlo*
tikin (TEE-keen) *adj.* dry; *seco*
tin tzéel (TEEN tzéehl) *prep. phr.* beside me (to my
 side); *al lado de mí*
ti' (tee') *prep.* in, on, with, to; *en, con, a*
ti'al (TEE'-ahl) *in. v.* belonging to; for; *suyo; para*
(ti')no'oh ([tee'] NOH'-oh) *n. phr.* right (to the);
 a la derecha
ti' te'ex (tee' TEH'-EHSH) *prep.* to you all; *a ustedes*
toh (toh) *adj.* direct, straight; *derecho, recto, directo*
tohol (TOH-hohl) *n.* price, value; *precio*
tok (tohk) *in. v.* burn; *quemar*
tokik (TOHK-eek) *tr. v.* lean; *inclinar*
tok' tuunich (tohk' TOOON-eech) *n.* flint, hard stone;
 pedernal, piedra dura
tóokik (TÓOHK-eek) *tr. v.* burn; *quemarlo*
tóolok (TÓOH-lohk) *n.* small lizard; *lagartija pequeña*
toon (toohn) *n.* penis; *pene, picha, verga*
tóotkóok (TÓOHT-kóohk) *n.* deaf-mute; *sordomudo*
to'ik (TOH'-eek) *tr. v.* cover, wrap; *cubrirlo*
to'on (toh'-ohn) *1st p. pl. pron.* us, we; *nosotros*
tuklik (TOOK-leek) *tr. v.* think; *pensarlo*
tuláakal (too-LÁAHK-ahl) *adj.* all; *todo*
tumen (TOO-mehn) *conj.* because; by; *porque; por*
tunkuluchú (toon-koo-loo-CHOO) *n.* owl; *tecolote,*
 búho; spelled alternatively **tunkuruchú**
(tu) paach ([too] paahch) *prep.* behind; *detrás de*
tupik (TOO-peek) *tr. v.* extinguish, put out (fire, light);
 kill; *apagarlo; matarlo*
tus beel (TOOS beehl) *n.* errand; *encargo*
tus beel (TOOS beehl) *tr. v.* commission; *comisionarlo*
tusbeltik (toos-BEHL-teek) *tr. v.* order; *mandarlo,*
 ordenarlo

tusik (TOOS-eek) *tr. v.* lie (to someone), deceive (someone); *mentirle, engañarlo*

tuucha (TOOOCH-ah) *n.* monkey; *mono*

tuukul (TOOOK-ool) *n.* thought, reason; *razón, pensamiento*

tuukul (TOOOK-ool) *in. v.* think; *pensar*

túumben (TÓOOM-behn) *adj.* fresh, new; *fresco, nuevo*

túun (tóoon) *adv.* then; *entonces*

tuunich (TOOON-eech) *n.* rock, stone; *piedra*

tuunkuy (TOOON-kooy) *n.* heel; *tacón, talón*

túunk'ul (TÓOON-k'ool) *n.* drum (horizontal); *tambor horizontál*

tuus (tooos) *n.* falsehood; *mentira*

tuus (tooos) *in. v.* lie; *mentir*

tuus (tooos) *tr. v.* deceive; *fingir, engañar*

túuxtik (TÓOOSH-teek) *tr. v.* send; *enviarlo*

tu'ub (too'-oob) *in. v.* forget; *olvidar*

tu'ubsik (TOO'-OOB-seek) *tr. v.* forget; *olvidarlo*

tu'ubul (TOO'-OOB-ool) *in. v.* forget; *olvidarse*

tu'ux (too'-oosh) *inter.* where?; *¿dónde?*

T'

t'aaham (T'AAH-hahm) *n.* callus, corn (on the body); *callo*

t'aan (t'aahn) *n.* language, speech, tongue; word; *idioma, lengua; palabra*

t'aan (t'aahn) *in. v.* speak; *hablar, decir*

t'abik (T'AHB-eek) *tr. v.* ignite, light; *encenderlo, incendiarlo*

t'anik (T'AHN-eek) *tr. v.* say; *hablarlo, llamarlo*

t'eel (t'eehl) *n.* comb (cock's); rooster; *cresta del ave; gallo*

t'iinil (T'EEEN-eel) *adj.* extended; tense, stiff; *tenso, tieso*

t'okik (T'OHK-eek) *tr. v.* cut (as in cutting fruit or leaves off a stem); gather; uproot; *cortarlo (como de cosechar fruta o cortar hojas de un palo); recoger, bajarlo; arrancarlo*

t'óon (t'óohn) *n.* calf (of the leg); *pantorilla de la pierna*

t'oxik (T'OSH-eek) *tr. v.* distribute, share; *repartirlo, distribuirlo*

t'o'ol (t'oh'-ohl) *n.* spine; *espinazo*

t'ubik (T'OOB-eek) *tr. v.* sink, submerge; *hundirlo, sumirlo*

t'uubul/t'ubukbal (T'OOO-bool/T'OO-book-bahl) *adj.* submerged, sunken; *hundido, sumido*

t'uup (t'ooop) *n.* little finger; *dedo meñique*

t'u'ul (T'OO'-ool) *n.* rabbit; *conejo*

TZ

tzaatz (tzaahtz) *n.* fat, grease; *unto, lo gordo de la carne*

tzáa'kaan (tzáah'-KAAHN) *n.* rattlesnake; *culebra tipo de cascabel*

tzahbil (TZAHB-eel) *adj.* fried; *frito*

tzahik (TZAH-heek) *tr. v.* fry; *freírlo*

tzakbesah (tzahk-BEH-sah) *tr. v.* add; *agregar, añadir, sumar*

tzayneh (TZAHY-neh) *tr. v.* follow; *seguirlo*

tzéel (tzéehl) *n.* side; *lado*

tzeentik (TZEEHN-teek) *tr. v.* feed; rear, nourish, support; *darle la comida; criar, mantener, apoyar*

tzíimin (TZÉEE-meen) *n.* horse; *caballo*

tzikbal (TZEEK-bahl) *tr. v.* chat; *platicar*

tzikbatik (TZEEK-baht-eek) *tr. v.* chat, discuss, recount, tell; show; *platicarlo, recontarlo; mostrarlo*

tzolik (TZOHL-eek) *tr. v.* explain; put in order; *explicarlo; ordenarlo*

tzo'otz (tzoh'-ohtz) *n.* hair; *pelo*

tzub (tzoob) *n.* agouti (*Dasyprocta punctata*); *agutí*

TZ'

tz'aak (tz'aahk) *n.* medicine; *medicina*

tz'aak se'en (tz'aahk SEH'-ehn) *n.* cold medicine; *medicina para catarro*

tz'akik (TZ'AHK-eek) *tr. v.* heal; *curarlo*

tz'a'ay (TZ'AH'-ahy) *n.* fang; *colmillo*

tz'íib (tz'éeeb) *n.* writing; *escritura*

tz'íib (tz'éeeb) *in. v.* write; *escribir*

tz'íiboltik (TZ'ÉEEB-ohl-teek) *tr. v.* imagine; wish, desire; *imaginarlo; desearlo*

tz'íibtik (TZ'ÉEEB-teek) *tr. v.* write; *escribirlo*

tz'íik (tz'éeek) *tr. v.* give; place, put; *darlo; ponerlo*

tz'íih k'ab (TZ'ÉEE k'ahb) *n.* left hand; *mano izquierdo*

tz'íis (tz'éees) *in. v.* copulate ("dirty" or crude connotation); *copular*

tz'ika'an (tz'ee-KAH'-ahn) *adj.* shaven; *afeitado*

tz'ikik (TZ'EEK-eek) *tr. v.* shave; *afeitarlo*

tz'oka'an (TZ'OHK-ah'-ahn) *adj.* done, ended, finished; *hecho, terminado, acabó*

tz'oka'an beel (TZ'OHK-ah'-ahn beehl) *in. v.* married (to be); *ser casado*

tz'onik (TZ'OHN-eek) *tr. v.* shoot; hunt; *dispararlo, tirarlo; cazar*

tz'on náal (TZ'OHN náahl) *n.* hunter; *cazador*

tz'ono'ot (TZ'OH-noh'-oht) *n.* sinkhole; *cenote*

tz'ook (tz'oohk) *n.* end, the last; leftover; *el fin, el último; sobrante*

tz'oon (tz'oohn) *n.* firearm, gun, shotgun; *arma de fuego, escopeta*

tz'oya'an (tz'oy-AH'-AHN) *adj.* skinny; *flaco*

tz'o'okol beel (tz'oh'-OHK-ohl BEEHL) *in. v.* marry; *casarse*

tz'o'oksik (TZ'OH'-OHK-seek) *tr. v.* finish; *terminarlo*

tz'o'om (tz'oh'-ohm) *n.* brains; marrow; pith; *sesos; medula*

tz'unu'un (TZ'OO-noo'-oon) *n.* hummingbird; *colibrí*

tz'uul (tz'oool) *n.* foreigner, stranger; white man/ woman; *extranjero; ladino*

tz'u'utz' (TZ'OO'-ootz') *in. v.* kiss; smoke; suck; *besar; fumar; chupar*

tz'u'utz'ik (TZ'OO'-ootz'-eek) *tr. v.* kiss; smoke; suck; *besar; fumarlo; chupar*

tz'u'uy (TZ'OO'-ooy) *adj.* hard, leathery, tough; *correoso, duro*

tz'u'uy pool (TZ'OO'-OOY poohl) *adj.* dumb, stupid; *estupido, tonto*

U

u hatz'il cháak (oo HAHTZ'-eel CHÁAHK) *n.* lightning, lightning bolt; *relámpago, rayo, rayo de cielo*

u ho'ol nah (oo HOH'-OHL nah) *n.* roof; *techo*

uk (ook) (hypothetical) *n.* seven; *siete*

uk' (ook') *n.* louse; *piojo*

uk'ah (OO-k'ah) *adj.* thirsty; *tener sed*

uk'ul (OOK'-ool) *in. v.* breakfast; drink; have; *desayunar; tomar*

u pool nah (oo POOHL nah) *n.* roof; *techo*

us (oos) *n.* gnat; *zancudito, jején*

ustik (OOS-teek) *tr. v.* blow (with mouth); *soplar algo con la boca*

u ta' kaax (OO tah' KAAHSH) *n.* droppings (chicken); *excremento de pollo*

u ta' miis (oo tah' MEEES) *n.* droppings (cat); *excremento de gato*

u ta' míis (ooh tah' MÉEES) *n.* sweepings; *basura barrida*

utz (ootz) *adj.* good, just; *bueno, justo*

utzkíintik (ootz-KÉEEN-teek) *tr. v.* improve, repair; *mejorarlo, repararlo*

úuchben (ÓOOCH-behn) *adj.* old, ancient; *antiguo*

úuchih (ÓOOCH-ee) *adv.* long ago; *anteriormente*

úuchul (ÓOOCH-ool) *in. v.* happen; *pasar, suceder*

úulum (ÓOO-loom) *n.* turkey (domesticated); *pavo*

úurich (ÓOOR-eech) *n.* snail (land); *caracol de tierra*

u yaal k'ab (oo YAAHL k'ahb) *n.* his/her finger; *dedo de el/ella*

u yeh (oo yeh) *n.* blade; point; *filo, afilado; punto*

u yeh kuchiiyoh (oo yeh koo-CHEEE-yoh) *n.* his knife blade; Sp. + Maya; *filo de cuchillo*

u ye'el toon (oo yeh'-ehl-TOOHN) *n.* testicles; *cojones, testículos*

u'uyik (OO'-OOY-eek) *tr. v.* feel; hear, listen; perceive; *sentirlo; oírlo, escucharlo; percibirlo*

W

waach (waahch) *n.* soldier; *soldado*

waah (waah) *n.* bread, tortilla; *pan, tortilla*

wáah (wáah) *inter.* if; *si, en caso de*

wáah ... wáah (wáah ... wáah) *inter.* either ... or; *o ... o*

wáah ba'ax (wáah BAH'-ahsh) *n.* something; *algo*

wáah máax (wáah MÁAHSH) *n.* someone; *alguien*

wáah tu'ux (wáah TOO'-oosh) *n.* somewhere; *algún lugar*

waak'al (WAAHK'-ahl) *adj.* burst; exploded; *reventado*

wáayhéel (WÁAHY-héehl) *n.* animal counterpart, spirit substitute; *nahual, espíritu*

wach'ik (WAHCH'-eek) *tr. v.* untie; *desatarlo, soltarlo*

wak (wahk) (hypothetical) *n.* six; *seis*

wak (wahk) *tr. v.* offer, expose; *ofrecer, exponer*

wakax (WAHK-ahsh) *n.* bull; cattle; cow; ox; *toro; ganado; vaca; buey*

wak'ik (WAHK'-eek) *n.* net hammock; *hamaca de red*

wak'ik (WAHK'-eek) *tr. v.* weave; *tejer*

wale' (WAH-leh') *adv.* maybe, perhaps; *tal vez, quizá*

watz'ik (WAHTZ'-eek) *tr. v.* bend ears of corn; *doblar el maíz*

waxak (WAH-shahk) (hypothetical) *n.* eight; *ocho*

wayak' (WAHY-ahk') *n.* dream; *sueño*

wayak' (WAHY-ahk') *in. v.* dream; *soñar*

waye' (WAH-yeh') *adv.* here; *aquí*

wayile' (wahy-EEL-eh') *n. phr.* local, native; *es de aquí*

wa'ak (wah'-ahk) *tr. v.* offered; *ofrecido*

wa'ak u bah (WAH'-AHK oo bah) *refl. v.* stand; *pararse*

wa'al (wah'-ahl) *in. v.* stop; stand up; *pararse; ponerse de pie*

wa'alen (WAH'-AHL-ehn) *imper.* stop!; *¡alto! ¡párate!*

wa'altal (WAH'-AHL-tahl) *imper.* stand up!; *¡pongase de pie!*

wa'bal (WAH'-bahl) *adj.* walking (on foot); still (not moving); stopped; *de pie; inmóvil; parado*

weech (WEEHCH) *n.* armadillo; *armadillo*

weehel/weekel (WEEH-hehl/WEEH-kehl) *adj.* spilled; *derramado*

wekik (WEH-keek) *tr. v.* spill; *derremarlo*

wekik ha' (WEH-keek HAH') *tr. v.* spill (water); *derramar agua*

wenel (WEHN-ehl) *in. v.* sleep; *dormir*

wíinik (WÉEEN-eek) *n.* man, person; *hombre, persona*

wíinkil (WÉEENK-eel) *n.* body; *cuerpo*

wiix (weeesh) *n.* urine; *orina*

wiix (weeesh) *in. v.* urinate; *orinar*

wi'ih (WEE'-ee) *adj.* hungry; *tener hambre*

wolis (WOHL-ees) *adj.* round; *redondo*

wóol a k'ab (wóohl AH k'ahb) *n.* fist; *puño*

wutz'ik (WOOTZ'-eek); *tr. v.* bend, fold; *plegarlo, doblarlo*

X

x (eesh) nominal honorific denoting feminine names, she of; *honorífico denotando nombres femeninos, ella de* ___

xáache' (SHÁAHCH-eh') *n.* comb; *peine*

xáachtik (SHÁAHCH-teek) *tr. v.* brush (one's hair); comb; *peinarse (el pelo)*

xaak (shaahk) *n.* basket (small); *canasta pequeña*

xáantal (SHÁAHN-tahl) *in. v.* stick around; delay, tarry; *tardarse, demorarse*

xamach (SHAH-mahch) *n.* griddle (for tortillas); *comal*

xaman (SHAH-mahn) *n.* north; *norte*

xaman ka'an (shah-mahn KAH'-AHN) *n.* north wind; *cierzo, viento del norte*

xan (shahn) *adv.* also; *también*

xanab (SHAH-nahb) *n.* footwear, sandal, shoe; *zapato, guarache*

xanal (SHAHN-ahl) *in. v.* late (to be); *tardarse*

xa'ak'tik (SHAH'-AHK'-teek) *tr. v.* mix up, jumble; *mezclarlo, revolverlo*

xa'an (shah'-ahn) *n.* palm thatch; *palmo para techo, guano*

xa'anil nah (SHAH'-AHN-eel NAH) *n.* thatched house; *casa de paja*

xa'anil p'ook (SHAH'-AHN-eel P'OOHK) *n.* straw hat; *sombrero de paja*

xch'úup (eesh-CH'ÓOOP) *n.* woman; *mujer*

xch'úupal (eesh-CH'ÓOOP-ahl) *n.* girl; *muchacha, niña*

xch'úupul xib (eesh-CH'ÓOOP-ool SHEEB) *n.* gay man (homosexual); *homosexual; maricón* (derogatory), *waco*

xeen (sheehn) *imper.* go!; *¡vaya!*

xeen te'elo' (sheehn TEH'-EH-loh') *imper.* beat it!, scram!; *¡váyate!*

xéet' (shéeht') *n.* bit, piece, portion; *pedazo*

xeh (sheh) *n.* vomit; *vómito*

xeh (sheh) *in. v.* vomit; *vomitar*

xiib (sheeeb) *n.* male, man; *varón, macho, hombre*

xiibil (sheeeb-eel) *n.* penis; *pene*

xiibil tzo'otz (sheeeb-eel TZOH'-OHTZ) *n.* man's hairstyle; *pelo de macho*

xiich' (sheeeech') *n.* tendon, sinew; nerve; *tendón; nervio*

xiik' (sheeek') *n.* armpit; wing; *sobaco; ala*

xíimbal (SHÉEEM-bahl) *in. v.* go, walk; *andar, caminar*

xíimbatik (SHÉEEM-BAHT-eek) *tr. v.* visit; *visitarlo*

xíiw (shéeew) *n.* herb (medicinal); *hierba (medicinal)*

xikik (SHEEK-eek) *tr. v.* break; crack; *reventarlo, quebrarlo, romperlo*

xikin (SHEE-keen) *n.* ear; *oreja*

xikin k'aak' (shee-keen K'AAHK') *n.* spark; *chispa*

xi'ik (shee'-eek) *in. v.* might go; *vaya*

xi'im (shee'-eem) *n.* corn; *maíz*

xi'ipal (SHEE'-EE-pahl) *n.* boy, youth; *muchacho, joven*

xkaax (EESH-kaahsh) *n.* hen; *gallina*

xkoonol (eesh-KOOH-nohl) *n.* vendor (female), saleswoman; *vendedora*

xk'áanho'ol (eesh-K'ÁAHN-hoh'-ohl) *n.* folded cloth used as pillow; *almohada de tela doblada*

xma' (EESH-mah') *prep.* lacking, without; *faltando, sin*

xma' nook' (EESH-mah' nook') *adj.* naked; *desnudo*

xnuuk (eesh-NOOOK) *n.* old woman; *vieja*

xok (shohk) *tr. v.* count; *contar*

xokik (SHOHK-eek) *tr. v.* count, read, study; *contarlo*

xook (shoohk) *tr. v.* read; *leer*

xotik (SHOH-teek) *tr. v.* cut, slice; *cortarlo*

xotik si' (SHOH-teek see') *tr. v.* cut firewood; *cortar leña*

xtáabay/xtabáay (eesh-TÁAH-bahy/eesh-TAH-báahy) *n.* female demon, female ghost; *duende feminino, demonio feminino, maligno feminino*

xt'uup (eesh-T'OOOP) *n.* sister (youngest); last female child in family; *hermana menor; última niña del familia*

xt'uut' (eesh-T'OOOT') *n.* parrot; *loro, perico*

xtz'aak (eesh-TZ'AAHK) *n.* female doctor, physician; *doctora, médica*

xunáan (SHOO-náahn) *n.* foreigner (female), stranger, woman (foreign); lady; white woman; *extranjera; ladina*

xúukum (eesh-ÓOO-koom) *n.* mourning dove; *paloma*

xuul (shoool) *n.* end; *cabo, fin*

xúul (shóool) *n.* stick (for planting), seeder; *coa, sembrador*

xuulab (SHOOO-lahb) *n.* ant (army); *hormiga soldado*

xuun (shooon) *n.* dear (what a husband calls his wife); *cariño*

xuupul (SHOOO-pool) *adj.* consumed, used up; *se gastó*

xuux (shooosh) *n.* wasp; *avispa*

xúux (shóoosh) *n.* basket (large); *canasta grande*

xuuxub (SHOOO-shoob) *in. v.* whistle; *chiflar, silbar*

xu'uk' (shoo'-ook') *n.* landmark, marker stones; corner of eye; *mojón, mojónes; rincon del ojo*

xu'upi (SHOO'-OO-pee) *adj.* used up; *gastado*

xu'upi (SHOO'-OO-pee) *par.* used up; *se gastó*

xwaach (eesh-WAAHCH) *n.* Mexican (female); *mexicána*

xwáay (eesh-WÁAHY) *n.* witch; *bruja*

xya'axkach (eesh-YAH'-AHSH-kahch) *n.* housefly; *mosca*

Y

yaah (yaah) *n.* hurt, pain; *dolor*

yaakuntik (yaah-KOON-teek) *tr. v.* love; *amarlo*

yaan (yaahn) *adv.* there is/there are; *hay*

yaan (yaahn) *in. v.* have; *tener*

yáanal (YÁAH-nahl) *adv.* below, beneath; *abajo, debajo de*

yáanal xiik' (YÁAH-nahl SHEEEK') *n.* armpit; *sobaco*

yáax (yáahsh) *prep.* first; prior; *primero; previo*

yáaxil (YÁAHSH-eel) *adj.* first; *primero*

yah (yah) *adj.* difficult, hard; painful; *difícil, duro; doloroso*

ya' (yah') *n.* sapote; *zapote*

ya'ab (yah'-ahb) *adj.* lot (a), much, many; *mucho(s)*

ya'abo'ob (YAH'-AHB-oh'-ohb) *phr.* they are many; *son muchos*

ya'akach (YAH'-AH-kahch) *adj.* many; *muchos*

ya'ax (yah'-ahsh) *adj.* blue; green; *azul; verde*

yeeb (yeehb) *n.* mist; fog; dew; *neblina, rocío*

yéetel (YÉEH-tehl) *prep.* with; together; *con; juntos*

yeex ko'olel (yeehsh KOH'-OHL-ehl) *n.* underpants; *pantaletas, calzónes*

yi'h (yee'h) *adj.* ripe (for the picking); *sazonado*

yi'htal (YEE'H-tahl) *tr. v.* ripen; *sazonarse*

yóon (YÓOHN) *n.* foam; *espuma*

yo'om (yoh'-ohm) *adj.* pregnant; *embarazada*

yo'omchahtal (yoh'-ohm-CHAH-tahl) *in. v.* pregnant (to become); *embarazarse*

yuntzil (YOON-tzeel) *pl. n.* forest spirit, invisible
spirits; *dueño del monte, espíritus invisibles*

yuuk (yoook) *n.* deer (small); fawn; *venado pequeño;
cervato*

yúultik (YÓOOL-teek) *tr. v.* polish, rub; *bruñirlo,
frotarlo*

yuum (yooom) *n.* father; gentleman; lord; man; god;
owner; *padre; caballero; señor; hombre; díos; dueño*

ENGLISH-MAYA
DICTIONARY

A

a (long thing) *adj.* huntz'íit (hoon-TZ'ÉEET); *un(a)*
(*cosa larga*)
a (person or animal) *adj.* huntúul (hoon-TÓOOL);
un(a) (persona o animal)
a (thing) *adj.* hump'éel (hoom-P'ÉEHL); *un(a) (cosa)*
a (tree) *adj.* hunkúul (hoon-KÓOOL); *un(a) (árbol)*
abandon *tr. v.* nak' (nahk'); *abandonar*
abdomen *n.* nak' (nahk'); *barriga, panza, estómago*
ability *n.* pat (paht); *habilidad, capacidad*
able, to be able to *adj.* páatal (PÁAH-tahl); *poder*
about to *prep.* ta'aytak (TAH'-AHY-tahck); *ya mero,*
inminente
above *adv., prep.* ka'anal (KAH'-AHN-ahl); *arriba*
abstain *in. v.* súuk'in bah (SÓOO-k'een BAH);
abstenerse
accept (a proposition) *tr. v.* ketik (KEH-teek); *aceptar*
(*una proposición*)
accident *n.* loob (loohb); *accidente*
accustomed *adj.* suuk (soook); *acostumbrado*
accustomed to (become) *tr. v.* naptzah (NAHP-tzah);
acostumbrarlo, habituarlo
achiote (red food dye; annatto) *n.* k'iwi' (K'EE-wee'),
k'uxu' (K'OO-shoo'); *achiote*
acidic *adj.* pah (pah); *ácido*
add *tr. v.* tzakbesah (tzahk-BEH-sah); *agregar,*
añadir, sumar
adjust *tr. v.* nuukbesah (noook-BEH-sah); *ajustar,*
arreglar, componer
adorn *tr. v.* senbesah (sehn-BEH-sah); *adornar,*
ornamentar
affair *n.* beel (beehl); *asunto*

afterward *adv.* ka'aka't(e') (KAH'-AH-kah'-t[e']); *al rato, un poco después, más tarde*
again *adv.* ka'ah (kah'-ah); *otra vez, de nuevo*
agave *n.* kih (kee); *maguey*
age *n.* (u) ha'abil ([oo] HAH'-AHB-eel); *edad*
age *in. v.* ch'iih (ch'eeeh); *hacer viejo*
agouti *(Dasyprocta punctata)* *n.* tzub (tzoob); *agutí*
air *n.* iik' (eeek'); *aire*
alive *adj.* kuxa'an (KOO-shah'-ahn); *vivo*
all *adj.* hóol (hóohl), láah (láah), tuláakal (too-LÁAHK-ahl); *todo*
alligator *n.* áayin (ÁAHY-een); *cocodrilo*
allow *tr. v.* cha' (chah'), cha(ik) (CHAH-[eek]); *dejar, permitir*
almost *adv.* asab (AH-sahb); *casi, por poco*
almost *prep.* ta'aytak (TAH'-AHY-tahck); *ya mero, inminente, casí*
a lot *adj.* hach ya'ab (HAHCH yah'-ahb); *mucho*
already *adv.* sáam (sáahm); *ya, listo*
already *adv.* tanilí (tahn-eel-EE); *ya, desde entonces, antes de ahora*
also *adv.* xan (shahn); *también*
altar *n.* ka'anche' (KAH'-AHN-cheh'), tem (tehm); *altar*
although *conj.* kex (kehsh); *aunque*
always *adv.* láayli'(e') (láahy-LEE'-[eh']); *siempre*
amuse *tr. v.* báaxal (BÁAHSH-ahl); *entretener, divertir*
ancient *adj.* úuchben (ÓOOCH-behn); *antiguo*
and *conj.* ka'ah (kah'-ah), yetel (YEH-tehl); *y*
angered *adj.* p'uuhul (P'OOO-hool); *enojado*
angry *adj.* k'áax (k'áahsh); *enojado*
animal (domestic) *n.* aalak' (AAHL-ahk'); *animal doméstico*
animal (wild) *n.* ba'alche' (BAH'-AHL-che'); *animal silvestre*
animal counterpart *n.* wáayhéel (WÁAHY-héehl); *nahual, espíritu*
annatto (red food dye; also *achiote*) *n.* k'iwi' (K'EE-wee'), k'uxu' (K'OO-shoo'); *achiote*
answer *tr. v.* núukik (NÓOOK-eek); *contestarlo, responderlo*
ant *n.* síinik (SÉEEN-eek); *hormiga*
ant (army) *n.* xuulab (SHOOO-lahb); *hormiga soldado*
ant (biting) *n.* popoxkan (poh-pohsh-KAHN); *hormiga que muerde*

anteater *n.* chab (chahb); *oso hormiguero*

anus *n.* iit (eeet); *ano*

anxious *aspect marker* taak (taahk); *ansioso*

anyone *pron.* he'e máax (heh'-eh MÁAHSH); *cualquier persona*

approach *in. v.* naatz'al (NAAHTZ'-ahl); *acercar*

approach *tr. v.* naatz'ik (NAAHTZ'-eek); *acercarlo*

arbor *n.* máakan (MÁAHK-ahn); *enramada*

area *n.* baanda (BAAHND-ah); *banda*

arise *in. v.* líik'il (LÉEEK'-eel); *levantarse*

arm *n.* k'ab (k'ahb); *brazo*

armadillo *n.* weech (WEEHCH); *armadillo*

armpit *n.* xiik' (sheeek'); *sobaco*

arrive *in. v.* k'uchul (K'OOCH-ool); *llegar*

ashamed *adj.* su'lak (SOO'-lahk); *avergüenzada*

ask for *tr. v.* k'áatik (K'ÁAHT-eek); *pedirlo, preguntarlo*

at *prep.* ti' (tee'); *en*

atole (corn gruel) *n.* sa' (sah'), saksa' (SAHK-sah'); *atole; atole con cáscara*

attain *tr. v.* chukik (CHOOK-eek); *alcanzarlo, conseguir*

avocado *n.* oon (oohn); *aguacate*

awake *n.* ahal (AH-hahl); *despierto*

awaken *in. v.* ahal (AH-hahl); *despertarse*

awaken *tr. v.* ahal (AH-hahl); *despertarlo*

ax *n.* báat (báaht); *hacha*

B

baby *n.* chaampal (chaahm-PAHL); *niño/niña, bebé*

back *n.* paach (paahch); *espalda, lomo*

bad *adj.* k'aas (k'aahs); *malo*

bag *n.* sáabukaan (SÁAH-boo-kaahn); *bolsa, morral*

bagasse (short fiber residue of henequin) *n.* so'oso'ok' (SOH'-OH-soh'-ohk') *bagazo*

bake *in. v.* tahal (TAH-hahl); *cocer por horno*

bake *tr. v.* tahal (TAH-hahl); *cocer por horno*

banana *n.* ha'as (hah'-ahs); *plátano*

bar-b-que pit *n.* píib (péeeb); *barbacoa, horno*

bark (tree) *n.* sóol (sóohl); *corteza*

base *n.* chuun (chooon), háal (háahl), iit (eeet); *raíz, principio; base*

basket (small) *n.* xaak (shaahk); *canasta pequeña*

basket (large) *n.* xúux (shóoosh); *canasta grande*

bat *n.* sootz' (soohtz'); *murciélago*

bathe *in. v.* ichkíil (EECH-kéeel); *bañarse*

bat (vampire) *n.* chikoop (CHEE-koohp); *murciélago de vampiro*

be able to *adj.* páatal (PÁAH-tahl); *poder*

beak *n.* koh (koh); *pico*

bean *n.* bu'ul (boo'-ool); *frijol*

bean (lima) *n.* iib (eeeb); *frijol de lima*

beard *n.* me'ex (meh'-ehsh); *barba*

beat *tr. v.* hatz'ik (HAHTZ'-eek); *golpearlo, azotarlo, pegarlo*

beat *in. v.* p'uuch (p'oooch); *batear*

beat it! *imper.* xeen te'elo' (sheehn-TEH'-EH-loh'); *¡váyate!*

beat (with a stick) *tr. v.* p'uchik (P'OOCH-eek); *golpearlo con palo*

beautiful *adj.* hatz'utz (HAHTZ'-ootz); *hermoso, bonito, bello*

beauty *n.* hatz'utzil (HAHTZ'-ootz-eel); *belleza*

because *conj.* tumen (TOO-mehn); *porque*

become accustomed to *tr. v.* naptzah (NAHP-tzah); *acostumbrarlo, habituarlo*

bedbug *n.* pik (peek); *chinche*

bee *n.* kaab (kaahb); *abeja*

beer *n.* cheba (CHEHB-ah); *cerveza*

beer (fermented honey) *n.* báalche' (BÁAHL-cheh'); *balche'*

before *prep.* táan (táahn); *delante, enfrente*

begin *tr. v.* chuunik (CHOOON-eek), káahsik (KÁAH-seek); *empezarlo, comenzarlo*

beginning *n.* chuun (chooon); *raíz, principio, origen*

behind *prep.* (tu) paach ([too] paahch); *detrás de*

belly *n.* nak' (nahk'); *barriga, panza, estómago*

belonging to *in. v.* ti'al (TEE'-ahl); *suyo*

below *adv.* kaabal (KAAHB-ahl), yáanal (YÁAH-nahl); *abajo*

belt *n.* k'axab nak' (K'AHSH-ahb nahk'); *cinturón*

bend *tr. v.* wutz'ik (WOOTZ'-eek); *plegarlo*

bend (ears of corn) *tr. v.* watz'ik (WAHTZ'-eek); *doblar el maíz*

beneath *adv.* yáanal (YÁAH-nahl); *debajo de*

beside me (to my side) *prep. phr.* tin tzéel (TEEN tzéehl); *al lado de mí*

big *adj.* nohoch (NOH-hohch), nuuktak (NOOOK-tahk); *gran, grande*

big (pl.) *adj.* nukuch (NOO-kooch); *grandes*

bird *n.* ch'íich' (ch'éeech'), mut (moot); *ave, pájaro*

bird (chachalaca) *n.* bach (bahch); *pájaro que se llaman "chachalaca"*

bit *n.* xéet' (shéeht'); *pedazo*

bit (a) *n.* hum p'íit (HOOM p'éeet); *un poco*

bite *in. v.* chi'ibal (CHEE'-EE-bahl); *morder*

biting *adj.* paapil (PAAHP-eel); *picante*

bitter *adj.* k'áah (k'áah); *amargo*

black *adj.* box (bohsh); éek' (éehk'); *negro*

blade *n.* u yeh (oo yeh); *filo, afilado*

blind *adj.* ch'op (ch'oohp); *ciego*

block (a road) *tr. v.* sup'ik (SOOP'-eek); *tapar (un camino)*

blocked (with poles) *adj.* sup'a'an (SOO-p'ah'-ahn); *cerrado (con palos)*

blond *adj.* chakxich' (CHAHK-sheech'), ch'el (ch'ehl); *güero*

blond child *n.* chan ch'el (CHAHN ch'ehl); *niño güero*

blood *n.* k'i'ik' (k'ee'-eek'); *sangre*

blow *n.* loobil (LOOHB-eel); *golpe*

blow (with mouth) *tr. v.* ustik (OOS-teek); *soplar algo con la boca*

blue *adj.* ya'ax (yah'-ahsh); *azul*

blue jay *n.* ch'el (ch'ehl); *arredajo*

boa constrictor *n.* och kaan (OHCH kaahn); *culebra tipo de boa*

boar *n.* kitam (KEE-tahm); *jabalí, puerco del monte (Pecari tajacu)*

boat *n.* cheem (cheehm); *barco*

body *n.* wíinkil (WÉEENK-eel); *cuerpo*

boil *in. v.* tahal (TAH-hahl); *hervir*

boil *tr. v.* tahal (TAH-hahl); *hervir*

bone *n.* bak (bahk); *hueso*

book *n.* hu'un (hoo'-oon); *libro*

born (to be) *in. v.* síihil (SÉEE-heel); *nacer*

borrowed *adj.* mahan (MAH-hahn); *prestado*

bosom *n.* iim (eeem); *seno, pecho*

boss *n.* noohoch-(il) (NOOH-hoch-[EEL]); *jefe*

bother *tr. v.* p'u'uhsik (P'OO'-OO-seek); *alborotarlo, molestarlo*

bothered *adj.* p'uuhul (P'OOO-hool); *molestado*

bottle gourd (*Legonaria siceraria*) *n.* chúuh (chóooh); *calabaza para llevar agua, calabaza vinatera*

bottom *n.* iit (eeet); *base*

bounce *in. v.* síit' (séeet'); *saltar, brincar*

bower *n.* máakan (MÁAH-kahn); *enramada*

boy *n.* pal (pahl); xi'ipal (SHEE'-EE-pahl); *niño; muchacho*

brains *n.* tz'o'om (TZ'OH'-ohm); *sesos*

branch *n.* k'ab (k'ahb); *rama*

bread *n.* waah (waah); *pan*

break *tr. v.* pa'ik (PAH'-eek); xikik (SHEEK-eek); *romperlo, quebrarlo; reventarlo*

breakfast (to have) *in. v.* uk'ul (OOK'-ool); *desayunar*

break (long things) *tr. v.* kachik (KAH-cheek); *quebrar cosas largas*

break out (in a rash) *tr. v.* íxbal (EESH-bahl); *tener roncha*

break wind *in. v.* kiis (keees); *echar pedos*

breast *n.* iim (eeem); *seno, pecho*

breathe *tr. v.* ch'a'iik'/ch'aik iik' (CH'AH'-eeek'/CH'AH-eek EEEK'); *respirar*

bring *tr. v.* ch'a'ik (CH'AH'-eek); taasik (TAAHS-eek); *traerlo*

broad *adj.* kóoch (kóohch); *ancho*

broken *adj.* kaacha'al (kaah-CHAH'-ahl); *quebrado*

broom *n.* míis (méees); *escoba*

broth *n.* k'aab/k'aa' (k'aahb/k'aah'), k'óol (k'óohl); *caldo*

brother (older) *n.* suku'un (SOO-koo'-oon); *hermano mayor*

brother (true sibling) *n.* láak'tzil (LÁAHK'-tzeel); *hermano verdadero*

brother (younger) *n.* íitz'in (ÉEETZ'-een); *hermano menor*

brother (youngest) *n.* ht'uup (ah-T'OOOP); *hermano menor*

bruise *in. v.* puch'ik (POOCH'-eek); *magullar*

brush *n.* k'áax (k'áahsh); *yerba, monte, bosque*

brush (one's hair) *tr. v.* xáachtik (SHÁAHCH-teek); *peinarse (el pelo)*

bucket *n.* ch'óoy (ch'óohy); *cubeta, cubo*

building *n.* nahil (NAH-eel); *edificio*

bull *n.* wakax (WAHK-ahsh); *toro*
bullfight *n.* pay wakax (pahy WAHK-ahsh); *torear,*
corrida de toros
burden *n.* kuuch (koooch); *carga*
burn *in. v.* elel (ehl-ehl), tok (tohk); *quemarse, arderse*
burn *tr. v.* tóokik (TÓOHK-eek); *quemarlo*
burst *in. v.* waak'al (WAAHK'-ahl); *reventar*
burst *tr. v.* xikik (SHEEK-eek); *reventarlo*
bury *tr. v.* mukik (MOOK-eek); *enterrarlo, sepultarlo*
busted *adj.* kaacha'al (kaah-CHAH'-ahl); *quebrado*
butterfly *n.* péepem (PÉEHP-ehm); *mariposa*
buttock *n.* bak'el iit (BAHK'-ehl EEET); p'u'ukil iit
(P'OO'-OOK-eel EEET); *nalga*
buy *tr. v.* manik (MAHN-eek); *comprarlo*
buzzard *n.* ch'oom (ch'oohm); *busardo*
by *conj.* tumen (TOO-mehn); *por*

C

cactus (prickly pear) *n.* páak'am (PÁAHK'-ahm);
nopal, tuna
caiman *n.* áayin (ÁAHY-een); *caimán*
calf (of the leg) *n.* t'óon (t'oohn); *pantorilla de
la pierna*
call *tr. v.* pay (pahy); *llamar*
callus *n.* t'aaham (T'AAH-hahm); *callo*
can *in. v.* ku páahtal (koo PÁAH-tahl); *se puede*
candle *n.* kib (keeb); *candela, vela*
candy *n.* ch'uhuk (CH'OO-hook); *dulce*
cane liquor (commercial) *n.* aanis (AAHN-ees);
Sp. loanword; *anís, aguardiente*
cannot *in. v.* ma' tu páahtal (mah' too PÁAH-tahl);
no se puede
canoe *n.* chem (chehm); *canoa*
canteen (bottle gourd) *n.* chúuh (chóooh); *calabaza
para llevar agua, calabaza vinatera*
cape (article of clothing) *adj.* háay (háahy); *capa*
captured *adj.* chuka'an (CHOO-kah'-ahn); *capturado*
care for (take care of) *tr. v.* kanantik (KAHN-ahn-
teek), ta'akik (TAH'-AHK-eek); *cuidarlo, guardarlo*
carry (on the back) *tr. v.* kuchik (KOOCH-eek);
cargarlo (en la espalda), llevarlo
case *n.* píix (péeesh); *caja, vaina*

cat *n.* miis (meees); *gato*

catarrh *n.* se'en (seh'-ehn); *catarro*

catch *tr. v.* chukik (CHOOK-eek); *alcanzarlo, pescarlo*

catch up (with someone) *tr. v.* chukpachtik (chook-PACH-teek); *alcanzar alguien*

cat droppings *n.* u ta' míis (oo tah' MÉEES); *excremento de gato*

catfish *n.* lu' (loo'); *bagre*

cattle *n.* wakax (WAHK-ahsh); *ganado*

cave *n.* aktun (AHK-toon); *cueva*

cavy (spotted) (rodent, *Cuniculus paca*) *n.* haaleb (HAAHL-ehb); *tapescuintle*

center *n.* chúumuk (CHÓOOM-ook); *centro*

change *tr. v.* k'exik (K'EHSH-eek); *cambiarlo*

changed *adj.* k'eexel (K'EEHSH-ehl); *cambiado, trocado*

charcoal *n.* chúuk (chóook); *carbón*

chat *tr. v.* tzikbal (TZEEK-bahl), tzikbatik (TZEEK-baht-eek); *platicar, platicarlo*

cheap *adj.* ma' ko'ohi' (MAH' koh'-oh-hee'); *barato*

chew *tr. v.* hach'ik (HAHCH'-eek); *mascarlo*

chicken *n.* kaax (kaahsh); *pollo*

chicken (baked) *n.* pibil kaax (PEEB-eel kaahsh); *pollo pibil*

chicken droppings *n.* u ta' kaax (OO tah' KAAHSH); *excremento de pollo*

chicken (fried) *n.* tzahbil kaax (TZAHB-eel KAAHSH); *pollo frito*

child *n.* chaampal (chaahm-PAHL), paal (paahl); *niño(a), bebé, menor*

chile *n.* iik (eeek); *chile, ají*

chin *n.* k'o no'och (K'OH noh'-ohch); *barbilla*

chocolate *n.* chukwa' (CHOOK-wah'); *chocolate*

cigar *n.* sáak' (sáahk'); *cigarra*

cigarette *n.* chamal (CHAHM-ahl); *cigarro, cigarrillo*

cistern *n.* ch'e'en (CH'EH'-ehn); *cisterna*

citrus fruit *n.* pak'áal (PAHK'-áahl); *cítricos*

claw *n.* íich'ak (ÉEE-ch'ahk); *uña*

clean *adj.* háanil (HÁAHN-eel); sak (sahk); *limpio*

clean *tr. v.* mistik (MEES-teek), utzkintik (OOTZ-keen-teek); *limpiarlo*

clear *adj.* sáas (sáahs); *claro*

clear *tr. v.* páak (páahk); *chapear, desherbar*

clear (of objects) *adj.* háanil (HÁAHN-eel); *limpio (de objetos)*

climb *tr. v.* na'akal (NAH'-AHK-ahl); *subir*

clitoris *n.* ak' (ahk'); *clítoris*

cloak *adj.* háay (háahy); *capa*

close *tr. v.* k'alik (K'AHL-eek), sup'ik (SOOP'-eek); *cerrarlo*

closed *adj.* k'aalal (K'AAHL-ahl); *cerrado*

clothes, clothing *n.* nook' (noohk'); *ropa*

cloud *n.* mu(n)yal (MOO[N]-yahl); *nube*

cloudy *adj.* nóokoy (NÓOHK-ohy); *nublado*

cloudy (liquid) *adj.* puuk (poook); *turbio*

coatimundi (*Nasua narica yucatanica*) *n.* chi'ik (chee'-eek); *coatimundi*

cob *n.* bakal (BAHK-ahl); *hueso del maíz, elote*

coffee *n.* boxha' (BOHSH-hah'), kaapeh (KAAH-peh); *café*

coil *tr. v.* to'ik (TOH'-eek); *rollarlo*

coil (rope) *tr. v.* kopik (KOH-peek); *enrollar soga*

cold *adj.* síis (séees); *frío*

cold *n.* se'en (seh'-ehn); *catarro*

cold medicine *n.* tz'aak se'en (tz'aahk SEH'-ehn); *medicina para catarro*

cold (meteorological) *adj.* ke'el (keh'-ehl); *frío*

comb *n.* xáache' (SHÁAHCH-eh'); *peine*

comb (cock's) *n.* t'eel (t'eehl); *cresta del ave*

comb *tr. v.* xáachtik (SHÁAHCH-teek); *peinarse (el pelo)*

come! *imp.* ko'oten (KOH'-OH-tehn); *¡vengase!*

come *in. v.* taal (taahl); *venir*

come out *in. v.* hóok'ol (HÓOHK'-ohl); *manifestarse*

commission *tr. v.* tus beel (TOOS beehl); *comisionarlo*

complete *adj.* chúuka'an (CHÓOOK-ah'-ahn); *completo*

complete *tr. v.* chukbesik (CHOOK-beh-seek); *completarlo, terminarlo*

completely *adv.* hum puli' (hoom POO-lee'); *completamente*

consumé (chicken) *n.* kaldo kaax (KAHL-doh KAAHSH); Sp. + Maya; *caldo de pollo*

consumed *adj.* xuupul (SHOOO-pool); *gastarse*

content *adj.* ki'imak óol (KEE'-EE-mahk ÓOHL); *contento*

convenient *adj.* ki' (kee'); *conveniente*

cook *in. v.*, *tr. v.* tahal (TAH-hahl); *cocer*

cook (as in beans) *in. v.* tah (tah); *madurarse, sazonarse*

cooked *adj.* tak'an (TAH-k'ahn); *cocido*

cooking pit (bar-b-que pit) *n.* píib (péeeb); *barbacoa, horno, pib*

cool *adj.* k'as ke'el (K'AHS keh'-ehl), síis (séees); *medio frio; frío*

copulate *in. v.* tz'íis (tz'éees); *copular*

corn *n.* xi'im (shee'-eem); *maíz*

corn (dough) *n.* sakan (SAHK-ahn); *masa*

corn (ear of) *n.* nal (nahl); *elote*

corner (of eye) *n.* xu'uk' (SHOO'-ook'); *rincon del ojo*

cornfield (personal) *n.* kool (koohl); *milpa*

cornmeal *n.* sakan (SAHK-ahn); *masa de maíz*

cornmeal beverage *n.* sa' (sah'), saksa' (SAHK-sah'); *atole, atole con cáscara*

corn (on the body) *n.* t'aaham (T'AAH-hahm); *callo*

cotton *n.* taman (TAH-mahn); *algodón*

cotton (combed) *n.* piitz' (peeetz'); *algodón desmotado*

cough (dry) *tr. v.* se'en (seh'-ehn); *toser*

count *tr. v.* xok (shohk); xokik (SHOHK-eek); *contar; contarlo*

cover *n.* píix (péeesh); *tapa, vaina*

cover *tr. v.* to'ik (TOH'-eek); *cubrirlo*

cow *n.* wakax (WAHK-ash); *vaca*

coyote *n.* ch'amak/ch'omak (CH'AHM-ahk/CH'OHM-ahk); *coyote*

crab *n.* bab (BAHB); *cangrejo*

crack *tr. v.* xikik (SHEEK-eek); *quebrarlo, romperlo*

crocodile *n.* áayin (ÁAHY-een); *cocodrilo*

crossed *adj.* k'aatal (K'AAH'-tahl); *cruzado*

crowded *adj.* babahkil (BAHB-ahk-eel); *atestado*

crush *in. v.* puch'ik (POOHCH'-eek); *despachurrar*

crush *tr. v.* petz'ik (PEHTZ'-eek); *apretar*

cry *in. v.* ok'ol (OHK'-ohl); *llorar*

curer *n.* hmeen (ah-MEEHN); *curandero*

curse *tr. v.* maldisyontik (MAHL-dees-yohn-TEEK); Sp. + Maya; *maldecirlo*

custard apple (soursop) *n.* óop (óohp); *anona*

cut *tr. v.* xotik (SHOH-teek); *cortarlo*

cut (as in cutting fruit or leaves off a stem) *tr. v.* t'okik (T'OHK-eek); *cortarlo*

cut brush *tr. v.* páaktik (PÁAHK-teek); *chapearlo*

cut firewood *tr. v.* xotik si' (SHOH-teek see');
cortar leña
cut with a blow *tr. v.* ch'akik (CH'AHK-eek); *cortarlo*
con un golpe
cut with scissors *tr. v.* k'osik (K'OHS-eek); *cortarlo*
con tijera
cyclone *n.* chak-ik'at (chahk-EEK'-aht); *huricán; ciclón*

D

daily *adv.* sáansamal (SÁAHN-sah-mahl); *diario,*
cada día
dance *n.* óok'ot (ÓOH-k'oht); *baile*
dance *in. v.* ok'ot (OH-k'oht); *bailar*
dangerous *adj.* hach k'aas u bin (HAHCH k'aahs oo
BEEN); *peligroso*
dark *adj.* ée'hoch'e'en (éeh'-HOHCH'-eh'-ehn); *oscuro*
dawn *n.* sáastal (SÁAHS-tahl); *amanecer*
day *n.* k'iin (k'eeen); *día*
day after tomorrow *n.* ka'abeh (KAH'-AHB-eh);
la mañana siguiente
dead *adj.* kimen (KEE-mehn); *muerto*
deaf *adj.* kóok (kóohk); *sordo*
deaf-mute *n.* tóotkóok (TÓOHT-kóohk); *sordomudo*
dear (what a husband calls his wife) *n.* xuun
(shooon); *cariño*
debris (from plants) *n.* sohol (SOH-hohl); *basura,*
basura de hojas secas
deceive *tr. v.* kechtik (KEHCH-teek); tusik (TOOS-eek);
tuus (tooos); *embaucarlo; engañarlo; fingir, engañar*
deep *adj.* taam (taahm); *profundo, hondo*
deer *n.* kéeh (kéeh); *venado*
deer (small) *n.* yuuk (yoook); *venado pequeño*
delay *in. v.* xáantal (SHÁAHN-tahl); *demorarse*
delicate *adj.* lukum (LOOH-koom); *delicado*
deliver *tr. v.* k'ubik (K'OOB-eek); *entregarlo*
demon (female) *n.* xtáabay/xtabáay (eesh-TÁAH-bahy/
eesh-TAH-báahy); *duende feminino, demonio*
feminino, maligno feminino
dense (become) *in. v.* su'utal (SOO'-OO-tahl); *espesar*
descend *in. v.* éemel (ÉEHM-ehl); *bajarse*
desire *tr. v.* tz'iiboltik (TZ'ÉEEB-ohl-teek); *desearlo*
detain *tr. v.* petz'ik (PEHTZ'-eek); *detener*

detest *tr. v.* p'ektik (P'EHK-teek); *odiarlo*

devil *n.* kisin (KEES-een); *diablo*

dew *n.* yeeb (yeehb); *rocío*

die *in. v.* kíimil (KÉEE-meel); *morir*

different *adj.* heel (heehl); hela'an (HEH-lah'-ahn); *diferente*

difficult *adj.* yah (yah); *difícil*

dig *tr. v.* páanik (PÁAHN-eek); *cavarlo*

digging stick *n.* lóob (lóohb); *coa*

dignity *n.* su'tal (SOO'-tahl); *dignidad*

diligent *adj.* séeb u meyah (SÉEHB ooh MEHY-ah); *diligente*

diminish *tr. v.* hatzik (HAHTZ-eek); *disminuir*

dinner *n.* o'och (OH'-ohch); *comida*

direct *adj.* toh (toh); *derecho, recto, directo*

direct/directly *adv.* naapul (NAAH-pool); *directo, inmediato*

dirt *n.* lu'um (loo'-oom); *suelo, tierra*

dirty *adj.* éek' (éehk'); *sucio*

disappear *in. v.* satpahal (saht-PAH-hahl); *desaparecerse*

discuss *tr. v.* tzikbatik (TZEEK-baht-eek); *platicarlo*

dislike *tr. v.* p'ektik (P'EHK-teek); *odiarlo*

disrobe *tr. v.* pitik (PEE-teek); *desnudarse, quitar la ropa*

distance *n.* náachil (NÁAHCH-eel); *distancia*

distant *adj.* náach (náahch); *lejos*

distinct *adj.* hela'an (HEH-lah'-ahn); *distinto*

distribute *tr. v.* t'oxik (T'OHSH-eek); *repartirlo, distribuirlo*

divide *tr. v.* hatzik (HAHTZ-eek); *dividirlo, partirlo*

do *tr. v.* betik (BEH-teek); *hacer*

doctor (female) *n.* xtz'aak (eesh-TZ'AAHK); *doctora, médica*

doctor (male) *n.* htz'aak (ah-TZ'AAHK); *doctor, médico*

dog *n.* peek' (peehk'); *perro*

doll *n.* aalnook' (AAHL-noohk'); *muñeca*

domestic animal *n.* aalak' (AAHL-ahk'); *mascota, animal doméstico*

domesticate *tr. v.* aalak'tik (aahl-AHK'-teek); *criarlo, crecerlo*

done *adj.* tz'oka'an (TZ'OHK-ah'-ahn); *hecho, terminado, acabó*

dove (mourning) *n.* xúukum (eesh-ÓOO-koom);
paloma

dream *n.* wayak' (WAHY-ahk'); *sueño*

dream *in. v.* náay (náahy); wayak' (WAHY-ahk'); *soñar*

drench *tr. v.* ch'ulik (CH'OOL-eek); *remojarlo*

dress *n.* nook' (noohk'); *ropa*

dress (native woman's) *n.* iipil (EEEP-eel); *huipil*

dress (put on clothes) *tr. v.* búukintik (bóoo-KEEN-teek); *vestirse, ponerlo ropa*

dried *adj.* hayk'inta'an (hahy-K'EEN-tah'-ahn); *seco*

drink *in. v.* uk'ul (OOK'-ool); *beber, tomar*

droppings (cat) *n.* u ta' míis (oo tah' MÉEES);
excremento de gato

droppings (chicken) *n.* u ta' kaax (OO tah' KAAHSH);
excremento de pollo

drum (horizontal) *n.* túunk'ul (TÓOON-k'ool); *tambor horizontál*

drunk *adj.* kala'an (KAH-lah'-ahn); *borracho*

drunk (to become) *in. v.* káaltal (KÁAHL-tahl);
emborracharse

dry *adj.* tikin (TEE-keen); *seco*

dry *in. v.* tihil (TEE-heel); *secarse*

dry *tr. v.* tihsik (TEE-seek); *secarlo*

dry (in the sun) *tr. v.* hayk'intik (hahy-K'EEN-teek);
secarlo (en el sol)

dumb *adj.* tz'u'uy pool (TZ'OO'-OOY poohl); *estúpido, tonto*

dusk *n.* bin ka ak'abtal (been kah AHK'-ahb-tahl);
anochecer

dye *n.* bon (bohn); *tinta, pintura*

E

eagle *n.* men (mehn); *aguila*

ear *n.* xikin (SHEE-keen); *oreja*

earlier *adv.* ka'ach (kah'-ahch); *antiguamente, entonces*

earlier today *adv.* behla'ak (BEH-lah'-ahk); *hoy anteriormente*

early *adv.* hatzkab k'iin (hahtz-kahb K'EEEN);
temprano, la mañana

earth *n.* kaab (kaahb), lu'um (loo'-oom); *tierra; mundo*

earth (white, used in mortar) *n.* sahkab/saskab (SAHK-ahb/SAHS-kahb); *roca calcárea deleznable, sascab*

east *n.* lak'in (LAH-k'een); *este, oriente*

eat *in. v.* hanal (HAHN-ahl); *comer*

eat *tr. v.* haantik (HAAHN-teek); *comerlo*

edge *n.* chi' (chee'); eh (eh); háal (háahl); *orilla; filo*

eel *n.* kaanilha' (kaahn-eel-HAH'); *anguila*

egg *n.* he' (heh'); *huevo*

eight *n.* waxak (WAH-shahk) (hypothetical); *ocho*

eight hundred *n.* ka' bak (KAH' bahk) (hypothetical); *ochocientos*

eight thousand *n.* hun pik (hoon PEEK) (hypothetical); *ocho mil*

eighty *n.* kan k'áal (KAHN k'áahl) (hypothetical); *ochenta*

either . . . or *inter.* wáah . . . wáah (wáah . . . wáah); *o . . . o*

elbow *n.* kúuk (kóook); *codo*

eleven *n.* buluk (BOO-look) (hypothetical); *once*

embarrassed *adj.* su'lak (SOO-lahk); *avergüenzada*

embarrassment *n.* su'utal (SOO'-OO-tahl); *vergüenza*

embrace *tr. v.* méek'ik (MÉEH-k'eek); *abrazarlo*

end *n.* tz'ook (tz'oohk), xuul (shoool); *el fin; cabo, fin*

ended *adj.* tz'oka'an (TZ'OHK-ah'-ahn); *terminado, acabó*

energy *n.* óol (óohl); *energía*

enough *adj.* hach ya'ab (HAHCH yah'-ahb); *bastante*

enter *in. v.* okol (OHK-ohl); *entrar*

entrance *n.* hool (hoohl); *entrada*

equal *aux. v.* éet (éeht); *igual, mismo*

errand *n.* tus beel (TOOS beehl); *encargo*

error *n.* siip/si'ip(il) (SEEEP/SEE'-EEP-[eel]); *error; yerro*

escape *in. v.* púutz'ul (PÓOOTZ'-ool); *escaparse*

evening *n.* oka'an k'iin (oh-KAH'-AHN k'eeen); *tarde*

evil *n.* k'aas (k'aahs); *mal, maldad*

exchange *tr. v.* k'exik (K'EHSH-eek); *cambiarlo*

exchanged *adj.* k'eexel (K'EEHSH-ehl); *trocar*

excrement *n.* ta' (tah'); *mierda, excremento, estiércol*

expect *tr. v.* pa'atik (PAH'-AHT-eek); *esperarlo*

expensive *adj.* ko'oh (koh'-oh); *caro*

explain *tr. v.* tzolik (TZOHL-eek); *explicarlo, ordenarlo*

explanation *n.* nu'ukul (NOO'-OOK-ool); *explicación*

explode *tr. v.* xikik (SHEE-keek); *reventarlo*

exploded *in. v.* waak'al (WAAHK'-ahl); *reventado*
expose *tr. v.* wak (wahk); *exponer*
extend *tr. v.* satz'ik (SAHTZ'-eek); *estirarlo*
extended *adj.* t'iinil (T'EEEN-eel); *tenso, tieso*
extinguish *tr. v.* tupik (TOO-peek); *apagarlo, matarlo*
extract *tr. v.* ho'osik (HOH'-OHS-eek); *sacarlo*
eye *n.* ich (eech); *ojo*

F

face *n.* ich (eech); *cara*
faded *adj.* poos (poohs); *descolorido, pálido, desteñido*
fair *adj.* chakxich' (CHAHK-sheech'); *güero*
fair complexioned *adj.* ch'el (ch'ehl); *güero*
falcon *n.* koos (koohs); *halcón*
fall *in. v.* lúubul (LÓOOB-ool); *caerse*
falsehood *n.* tuus (tooos); *mentira*
fang *n.* tz'a'ay (TZ'AH'-ahy); *colmillo*
farm *n.* kol (kohl); *milpa*
farmer *n.* koolnáal (KOOHL-náahl); *milpero*
fat *adj.* polok (POHL-ohk); *gordo*
fat *n.* tzaatz (tzaahtz); *unto, lo gordo de la carne*
father *n.* taat(ah) (TAAHT-[ah]), yuum (yooom),
    paapah (PAAH-pah); Sp. loanword; *papá, padre*
fault *n.* kuch (kooch); siip/si'ip(il) (SEEEP/
    SEE'-EEP-[eel]); *culpa*
fawn *n.* yuuk (yoook); *venado pequeño; cervato*
fear *n.* saahkil (SAAHK-eel); *miedo, temor*
feathers *n.* k'u'uk'um (k'oo'-ook'-OOM); *plumas*
feed *tr. v.* tzeentik (TZEEHN-teek); *darle la comida*
feel *tr. v.* u'uyik (OO'-OOY-eek); *sentirlo*
fence in (with poles or posts) *tr. v.* sup'ik (SOOP'-
    eek); *cercar con postes o palos*
fever *n.* chokwil (CHOHK-weel); *calentura*
field *n.* kol (kohl); *milpa*
fifteen *n.* ho' lahun (HOH' LAH-hoon) (hypothetical);
    quince
fifty-fifty *adj.* chunchumuk (choon-CHOO-mook);
    mitad y mitad
fight *n.* ba'te'el (BAH'-teh'-ehl); *pelea, problema*
fight *tr. v.* ba'te'el (BAH'-teh'-ehl); *pelear*
file *n.* eh (eh); *filo*

fill *tr. v.* but'ik (BOOT'-eek), chupik (CHOOP-eek); *llenarlo*

filled *adj.* chuupul (CHOOOP-ool); *hinchado*

find *tr. v.* kaxtik (KAHSH-teek); *hallarlo*

find out *tr. v.* oheltik (oh-HEHL-teek); *reconocerlo, enterarse de*

fine *adj.* lukum (LOOK-oom); *fino*

finger *n.* aal k'ab (aahl k'ahb), u yaal k'ab (oo YAAHL k'ahb); *dedo*

finger (little) *n.* t'uup (t'ooop); *dedo meñique*

fingernail *n.* íich'ak (ÉEE-ch'ahk); *uña*

finish *tr. v.* chukbesik (CHOOK-beh-seek), tz'o'oksik (TZ'OH'-OHK-seek); *completarlo, terminarlo*

finished *adj.* chúuka'an (CHÓOOK-ah'-ahn), tz'oka'an (TZ'OHK-ah'-ahn); *terminado*

fire *n.* k'áak' (k'áahk'); *fuego*

firearm *n.* tz'oon (tz'oohn); *arma de fuego*

firewood *n.* si' (see'); *leña*

firm *adj.* hetz'a'an (HEHTZ'-ah'-ahn); *firme, asentado, fundado*

first *adj.* yáaxil (YÁAHSH-eel); *primero*

first *prep.* yáax (yáahsh); *primero*

fish *n.* kay (kahy); *pescado*

fist *n.* wóol a k'ab (wóohl AH k'ahb); *puño*

five *n.* ho' (hoh'); *cinco*

fixed *adj.* hetz'a'an (HEHTZ'-ah'-ahn); *firme, asentado, fundado*

flail *tr. v.* p'uchik (P'OOCH-eek); *desgranar*

flail (grain or fruit) *in. v.* p'uuch (p'oooch); *batear*

flat *adj.* pek'a'an (PEH-K'AH'-ahn), táax (táahsh); *llano, plano*

flatten *tr. v.* mach' (mahch'); *allanar, aplanar, aplastar*

flatten *tr. v.* pak'achtik (PAHK'-ahch-teek); *hacerlo*

flatulence *n.* kiis (keees); *pedo*

flint *n.* tok' tuunich (tohk' TOOON-eech); *pedernal*

flour (corn) *n.* sakan (SAHK-ahn); *harina de maíz*

flower *n.* lool (loohl); *flor*

flower (frangipani) *n.* nikte' (NEEK-teh'); *flor*

flute *n.* piito (PEEE-toh); Sp. loanword; *pito, flauta*

fly (house) *n.* xya'axkach (eesh-YAH'-AHSH-kahch); *mosca*

foam *n.* yóon (yóohn); *espuma*

fog *n.* yeeb (yeehb); *neblina*

fold *tr. v.* wutz'ik (WOOTZ'-eek); *doblarlo*

follow *tr. v.* tzayneh (TZAHY-neh); *seguirlo*

food *n.* hanal (HAHN-ahl); *comida*

fool *tr. v.* kechtik (KEHCH-teek); *embaucarlo*

foot *n.* ook (oohk); *pie*

footwear *n.* xanab (SHAH-nahb); *zapato, guarache*

for *in. v.* ti'al (TEE'-ahl); *para*

forceful *adj.* muuk' (moook'); *fuerte*

foreigner *n.* tz'uul (tz'oool); *extranjero, ladino*

foreigner (female) *n.* xunáan (SHOO-náahn); *extranjera, ladina*

forest *n.* k'áax (k'áahsh); *selva, monte, bosque*

forest spirit *n.* yuntzil (yoon-TZEEL); *dueño del monte*

forest (virgin) *n.* suhuy k'áax (SOO-hooy K'ÁAHSH); *monte virgen (nunca labrada)*

forget *in. v.* tu'ub (too'-oob), tu'ubul (TOO'-OOB-ool); *olvidar; olvidarse*

forget *tr. v.* tu'ubsik (TOO'-OOB-seek); *olvidarlo*

forty *n.* ka' k'áal (KAH' k'áahl) (hypothetical); *cuarenta*

fountain *n.* sayab (SAHY-ahb); *fuente*

four *n.* kan (kahn); *cuatro*

four hundred *n.* hun bak (HOON bahk) (hypothetical); *cuatrocientos*

four (inanimate things) *adj., pron.* kamp'éel (kahm-P'ÉEHL); *cuatro (cosas)*

four (people or animals, animate things) *adj., pron.* kantúul (kahn-TÓOOL); *cuatro (personas o animales)*

fourteen *n.* kan lahun (kahn LAH-hoon) (hypothetical); *catorce*

fox *n.* ch'amak/ch'omak (CH'AH-mahk/CH'OH-mahk); ooch (oohch); *zorro*

fracture (long things) *tr. v.* kachik (KAH-cheek); *fracturar (cosas largas)*

fractured *adj.* kaacha'al (kaah-CHAH'-ahl); *fracturado*

frangipani (flower) *n.* nikte' (NEEK-teh'); *frangipaniero*

free *tr. v.* cha' (chah'); *dejar libre*

freeze *tr. v.* síiskuntik (SÉEES-koon-teek) *enfriarlo*

fresh *adj.* aak' (aahk'), túumben (TÓOOM-behn); *fresco, nuevo*

fresh meat *n.* aak' bak' (AAHK' bahk'); *fresco*

fried *adj.* tzahbil (TZAHB-eel); *frito*

friend *n.* áamigoh (áah-MEE-goh); Sp. loanword; *amigo*

frighten *tr. v.* sahahkúuns (SAH-hah-kóoons);
   asustarlo, espantarlo
frightened *adj.* p'uuhul (P'OOO-hool); *espantado*
frightening *adj.* hak'óolal (hah-K'ÓOOL-ahl); *con susto*
frog *n.* muuch (moooch); *rana*
from *prep.* tak (tahk); *de, desde*
front *n.* táan (táahn); *frente*
front of (in) *prep.* táanil (TÁAHN-eel); *enfrente de*
fruit *n.* ch'uhuk (CH'OOH-hook); *fruta*
fry *tr. v.* tzahik (TZAH-heek); *freírlo*
full *adj.* chuup (chooop); *lleno*

G

gather *tr. v.* t'okik (T'OHK-eek); *recoger, bajarlo*
gay (homosexual) *n.* xch'úupul xib (eesh-CH'ÓOOP-
   ool SHEEB); *maricón* (derogatory), *waco*
gentleman *n.* yuum (yooom); *caballero, señor*
get away *in. v.* púutz'ul (PÓOOTZ'-ool); *escaparse*
get drunk *in. v.* kaltal (KAHL-tahl); *emborracharse*
get lost *in. v.* satpahal (saht-PAH-hahl); *desaparecerse*
get started *in. v.* chunpahal (choon-PAH-hahl);
   empezarse, comenzar
get up in/on *tr. v.* na'akal (NAH'-AHK-ahl); *subir*
ghost (female) *n.* xtáabay/xtabáay (eesh-TÁAH-bahy/
   eesh-TAH-báahy); *duende feminino, demonio*
   feminino, maligno feminino
gift *n.* síihbil (SÉEEB-eel); *regalo*
girl *n.* xch'úupal (eesh-CH'ÓOOP-ahl); *muchacha, niña*
give *tr. v.* tz'íik (tz'éeek); *darlo, ponerlo*
give (as a gift) *tr. v.* síihik (SÉEE-heek); *regalarlo*
gnat *n.* us (oos); *zancudito, jején*
go *in. v.* hóok'ol (HÓOHK'-ohl), bin (been), xíimbal
   (SHÉEEM-bahl); *salir, irse, andar*
go! *imper.* xeen (sheehn); *¡vaya!*
goad *n.* aach (aahch); *ramal*
goat *n.* htaman (ah-TAH-mahn); *chivo, cabro*
god *n.* yuum (yooom); *dios*
gods *pl. n.* k'uho'ob (K'OO-hoh'-ohb); *dioses*
gold *n.* taak'in (TAAH-k'een); *oro*
go (might) *in. v.* xi'ik (shee'-eek); *vaya*
good *adj.* ma'alob (mah'-AHL-ohb), utz (ootz);
   bien, bueno

good-looking *adj.* ki'ichpam (KEE'-EECH-pahm); *hermoso, guapo*

goodness *n.* hatz'utzil (HAHTZ'-ootz-eel); *bondad*

good (very) *adj.* hatz'utz (HAHTZ'-ootz), sen ma'alob (sehn MAH'-AHL-ohb); *muy bien, buenísimo*

go out *in. v.* hok'ol (HOHK'-ohl); *manifestarse*

gourd (bottle) (*Legonaria siceraria*) *n.* chúuh (chóooh); *calabaza para llevar agua, calabaza vinatera*

gourd (from a tree) *n.* luuch (loooch); *jícara, calabaza de árbol*

gourd (large) *n.* homa' (HOH-mah'); *calabaza/jícara grande*

grab *tr. v.* machik (MAHCH-eek); *agarrarlo*

grandchild *n.* áabil (ÁAH-beel); *nieto*

grandfather *n.* nohoch taat(ah) (NOH-hohch TAAHT-[ah]); *abuelo*

grandfather (aged) *n.* mam (mahm); *abuelo viejo*

grandmother *n.* chiich (cheeech); *abuela*

grasp *tr. v.* machik (MAHCH-eek); *asirlo*

grass *n.* su'uk (soo'-ook); *zacate*

grease *n.* tzaatz (tzaahtz); *unto, lo gordo de la carne*

green *adj.* ya'ax (yah'-ahsh); *verde*

green corn *n.* áak'nal (ÁAHK'-nahl); *maíz verde*

green corn gruel *n.* áak'sa' (ÁAHK'-sah'); *atole de maíz tierno, atole nuevo*

green (immature) *adj.* áak' (áahk'); *fresco, verde (immaduro)*

griddle (for tortillas) *n.* xamach (SHAH-mahch); *comal*

griddle (iron) *n.* máaskabil xamach (máahs-KAHB-eel SHAH-mahch); *comal de hierro*

grill *tr. v.* k'a'atik (K'AH'-AH-teek); *asarlo*

grilled *adj.* k'a'bil (K'AHB'-eel); *asado*

grilled (meat) *n.* k'a'bil bak' (K'AHB'-eel BAHK'), pok chuk (POHK chook); *carne asada*

grime (around collar) *in. v.* kiiritz' (KEEER-eetz'); *mugre*

grind *in. v.* puch'ik (POOCH'-eek); *moler*

grind *tr. v.* huch'ik (HOOCH'-eek); *molerlo*

grinding stone *n.* ka'ah (kah'-ah); *metate*

grind (lime-soaked corn) *tr. v.* huch' k'u'um (HOOCH' k'oo'-oom); *moler nixtamal/masa*

ground *adj.* huch'bil (HOOCH'-beel); *molido*

ground (into meal) *adj.* muxbil (MOOSH-beel); *molido*

grow *tr. v.* aalak'tik (aahl-AHK'-teek); *criarlo, crecerlo*

grown *in. v.* ch'iihil (CH'EEE-heel); *crecer*

gruel *n.* k'eyem (K'EH-yehm); *pozole*

gruel (corn) *n.* saksa' (SAHK-sah'), sa' (sah'); *atole, atole con cáscara*

guava *n.* pichi' (PEECH-ee'); *guayaba*

gun *n.* tz'oon (tz'oohn); *escopeta*

H

hail *n.* bat (baht); *granizo*

hair *n.* ho'ol (hoh'-ohl), tzo'otz (tzoh'-ohtz), u tzo'tze a ho'ol (OO tzoh'-tzeh ah HOH'-ohl); *pelo*

hairstyle (man's) *n.* xiibil tzo'otz (sheeeb-eel TZOH'-OHTZ); *pelo de macho*

half *adj.* chumuk (CHOO-mook); *medio*

hammock *n.* k'áan (k'áahn); *hamaca*

hammock (net) *n.* wak'ik (WAHK'-eek); *hamaca de red*

hand *n.* k'ab (k'ahb); *mano*

hand (left) *n.* tz'íih k'ab (TZ'ÉEE k'ahb); *mano izquierdo*

hang *tr. v.* ch'uytal (CH'OOY-tahl); *colgarlo*

hang (fruit) *in. v.* ch'úuyul (CH'ÓOOY-ool); *colgarse fruta*

hang (up) *tr. v.* sinik (SEEN-eek); *guindarlo, colgarlo*

happen *in. v.* úuchul (ÓOOCH-ool); *pasar, suceder*

happy *adj.* ki'imak óol (KEE-EE-mahk ÓOHL); *contento*

hard *adj.* tz'u'uy (TZ'OO'-ooy); yah (yah); *duro*

harsh *adj.* k'a'am (K'AH'-ahm); *recio, fuerte*

harvest *in. v.* hooch (hoohch); *cosechar*

harvest *tr. v.* hochik (HOHCH-eek); *cosecharlo*

hat *n.* p'ok (p'ohk); *sombrero*

hatchet *n.* báat (báaht); *hacha*

hate *tr. v.* p'ektik (P'EHK-teek); *odiarlo*

hated *par.* (with agent) p'eeka'an (p'eeh-KAH'-AHN); *aborrecido, abominado*

hateful *adj.* k'áax (k'áahsh); *odioso*

hat (straw) *n.* xa'anil p'ook (SHAH'-AHN-eel P'OOHK); *sombrero de paja*

have *in. v.* uk'ul (OO-k'ool); yaan (yaahn); *tener*

hay *n.* su'uk (SOO'-ook); *zacate*

head *n.* ho'ol (hoh'-ohl); pool (poohl); *cabeza*

headache *n.* k'inan (in) ho'ol' (K'EEN-ahn een HOH'-OHL'); *dolor de cabeza*

heal *tr. v.* tz'akik (TZ'AHK-eek); *curarlo*

hear *tr. v.* u'uyik (OO'-OOY-eek); *oírlo*

heart *n.* óol (óohl); puksi'ik'al (POOK-see'-eek'-ahl); *corazón*

hearth *n.* k'ooben (K'OOH-behn); *fogón*

heat *tr. v.* chokokúuntik (choh-koh- KÓOON-teek); *calentarlo*

heated up *adj.* k'íinal (K'ÉEE-nahl); *calientado*

heaven *n.* ka'an (kah'-ahn); *cielo*

heavy *adj.* al (ahl); *pesado*

heel *n.* tuunkuy (TOOON-kooy); *tacón, talón*

help *in. v.* áantah (ÁAHN-tah); *ayudar*

help *tr. v.* áantik (ÁAHN-teek); *ayudarlo*

helper *n.* aantah (AAHN-tah); *ayudante*

hemp (sisal) *n.* kih (kee); *henequén, maguey*

hen *n.* xkaax (EESH-kaahsh); *gallina*

herbalist *n.* hmeen (ah-MEEHN); *curandero, yerbatero*

herb (medicinal) *n.* xíiw (shéeew); *hierba (medicinal)*

here *adv.* te' (teh'); waye' (WAH-yeh'); *aquí*

here/there it is *dem.* he'el(a')/(o') (HEH'EHL-[ah']/ [oh']); *aquí/allí está* (a' = close, o' = further away)

heron (white) *n.* sak bok (SAHK bohk); *garza blanca*

hide *tr. v.* ta'akik (TAH'-AHK-eek); *esconderlo*

hide (skin) *n.* k'éewel (K'ÉEH-wehl); *piel, pellejo, cuero*

high *adj.* ka'anal (KAH'-AHN-ahl); *arriba, alto*

hill *n.* muul (moool); *cerro*

hit *tr. v.* hatz'ik (HAHTZ'-eek); *golpearlo, pegarlo*

hoarse *adj.* ma'a kaal (MAH'-AH kaahl); *ronco*

hole *n.* hool (hoohl); *hoyo, hueco*

hollow *adj.* poos (poohs); *waco*

home *n.* nahil (NAH-eel); otoch (oh-tohch); *casa; hogar*

homosexual (man) *n.* xch'úupul xib (eesh-CH'ÓOOP- ool SHEEB); *maricón* (derogatory), *waco*

honey *n.* kaab (kaahb); *miel*

horn *n.* bak (bahk); *cuerno*

horse *n.* tzíimin (TZÉEE-meen); *caballo*

hot *adj.* chokoh (CHOHK-oh); k'íinal (K'ÉEE-nahl); *caliente*

hot (become) *in. v.* chokotal (chohk-oh-TAHL); *calentarse*

hot (spicy) *adj.* páap (páahp); *picante*

hot (weather) *adj.* k'íilkab (K'ÉEEL-kahb); *(hace) calor*

house *n.* nah (nah); *casa*

how? *inter.* bíix (béeesh); *¿como?*

humid (weather) *adj.* k'íilkab (K'ÉEEL-kahb); *humido*
humiliate oneself *refl.* ta'ik u bah (TAH'-eek oo bah);
   defecarse (literally, "defecate on oneself")
hummingbird *n.* tz'unu'un (TZ'OO-noo'-oon); *colibrí*
hungry *adj.* wi'ih (WEE'-ee); *tener hambre*
hunt *tr. v.* tz'onik TZ'OHN-eek); *cazar*
hunter *n.* tz'on náal (TZ'OHN náahl); tz'onero (tz'ohn-
   ER-oh); *cazador*
hurricane *n.* chakik'at (chahk-EEK'-aht); chichiik'
   (CHEECH-eeek'); *huricán, ciclón*
hurry *in. v.* séeb (séehb); séekuntik (SÉEH-koon-teek);
   rápido; estar de prisa
hurt *n.* yaah (yaah); *dolor*
hurt *in. v.* chi'ibal (CHEE'-EE-bahl); *doler*
hurt *tr. v.* kinbesik (keen-BEH-seek); *herirlo*
hurt (oneself) *in. v.* kinpahal (keen-PAH-hahl); *herirse*
husband *n.* iicham (EEECH-ahm); *marido, esposo*
husk *n.* sóol (sóohl); *carapacho*

I

I *1st p. s. pron.* teen (teehn); *yo*
if *inter.* wáah (wáah); *si, en caso de*
ignite *tr. v.* t'abik (T'AHB-eek); *encenderlo, incendiarlo*
ignorant *adj.* nuum (nooom); *estúpido*
iguana *n.* huuh (hoooh); *iguana*
illness *n.* k'oha'anil (k'oh-HAH'-AHN-eel); *enfermedad*
ill (to become) *in. v.* k'oha'antal (k'oh-HAH'-AHN-
   tahl); *enfermarse*
imagine *tr. v.* tz'íiboltik (TZ'ÉEEB-ohl-teek);
   imaginarlo
immediately *adv.* beoritasa (BEH-oh-ree-TAH-sah),
   naapulak (naah-POOL-ahk); *en seguido*
important *adj.* k'a'ana'an (K'AH'-AH-nah'-ahn);
   importante
improve *tr. v.* utzkíintik (ootz-KÉEEN-teek); *mejorarlo*
in *prep.* ti' (tee'); ichil (EECH-eel); *en; dentro*
incline *n.* níix (néeesh); *inclinación*
indeed *adv.* he'ele' (HEH'-EHL-eh'); *sí, claro*
Indian *n.* máasewáal (máah-SEH-wáahl); *indígena,
   mazehual; inferior*
infant *n.* paal (paaahl); *niño(a), nene*

inferior *n.* máasewáal (máah-SEH-wáahl); *inferior;*
indígena, mazehual
injury *n.* loob (loohb); *daño, herrida*
insert *tr. v.* oksik (OHK-seek); *introducirlo, meterlo*
inside *prep.* ichil (EECH-eel); *dentro*
intact *adj.* suhuy (SOO-hooy); *intacto; virgen*
intestines *n.* chooch (choohch); *intestinos, tripas*
intoxicated *adj.* kala'an (KAH-lah'-ahn); *borracho*
introduce *tr. v.* oksik (OK-seek); *introducirlo, entrar,*
hacerlo
iron *n.* máaskab (MÁAHS-kahb); *hierro*
iron griddle *n.* máaskabil xamach (máahs-KAHB-eel
SHAH-mahch); *comal de hierro*
itch/itching *n.* saak' (saahk'); *comezón*

J

jaguar *n.* balam (BAH-lahm); chakmo'ol (chahk-
MOH'-OHL); koh (koh); *jaguar, tigre*
jay *n.* ch'el (ch'ehl); *arredajo*
jicama (edible plant) *n.* chi'ikam (CHEE'-EEK-ahm);
jícama
joke *in. v.* báaxal (BÁAHSH-ahl); *bromear*
juice *n.* k'aab/k'aa' (k'aahb/k'aah'); *jugo*
jumble *tr. v.* xa'ak'tik (SHAH'-AHK'-teek); *mezclarlo,*
revolverlo
jump *in. v.* sit' (seet'); *brincar*
jungle *n.* k'áax (k'áahsh); *selva, monte, bosque*
just *adj.* utz (ootz); *justo*

K

keep *tr. v.* ta'akik (TAH'-AHK-eek); *guardarlo*
kill *tr. v.* kíinsik (KÉEENS-eek); tupik (TOO-peek);
matarlo
kiss *in. v.* tz'u'utz' (TZ'OO'-ootz'); *besar*
kiss *tr. v.* tz'u'utz'ik (TZ'OO'-ootz'-eek); *besar*
kitchen *n.* k'ooben (K'OOH-behn); *cocina*
knee *n.* píix (péeesh); *rodilla*
knife blade (his) *n.* u yeh kuchiiyoh (oo yeh koo-
CHEEE-yoh); Sp. + Maya; *filo de cuchillo*

know *tr. v.* kanik (KAHN-eek), oohel (OOH-hehl), ohéeltik (oh-HÉEHL-teek); *saberlo, conocerlo; reconocerlo, notar*
know (someone) *tr. v.* k'ahóol (K'AH-hóohl); *conocerlo*

L

lacking *prep.* xma' (EESH-mah'); *faltando*
lady *n.* xunáan (SHOO-náahn); *dama*
lagoon *n.* aak'al (AAHK'-ahl); *laguna*
lake *n.* ha' (hah'); *laguna*
landmark *n.* xu'uk' (SHOO'-ook'); *mojón*
land (unit of 20 x 20 m) *n.* p'isik'an (P'EES-eek'-ahn); *mecate*
language *n.* t'aan (t'aahn); *idioma, lengua*
large *adj.* nohoch (NOH-hohch); *gran, grande*
large (pl.) *adj.* nukuch (NOO-kooch); *grandes*
lasso *n.* suum (sooom); *lazo*
last (the) *n.* tz'ook (tz'oohk); *el último*
later *adv.* ka'aka't(e') (KAH'-AH-kah'-t[e']); *al rato, un poco después, más tarde*
late (to be) *in. v.* xanal (SHAHN-ahl); *tardarse*
laugh *in. v.* che'eh (cheh'-eh); *reírse*
laughter *n.* che'eh (cheh'-eh); *risa*
lazy *adj.* nuum (nooohm); *perezoso*
lazy man *adj.* hoykeep (HOHY-keehp); *hombre flojo*
leaf *n.* le' (leh'); *hoja*
league (measure) *n.* lúub (lóoob); *legua*
lean *tr. v.* tokik (TOHK-eek); *inclinar*
learn *tr. v.* kanik (KAHN-eek); *aprenderlo*
leather *n.* k'éewel (K'ÉEH-wehl); *cuero*
leathery *adj.* tz'u'uy (TZ'OO'-ooy); *correoso*
leave *in. v.* hóok'ol (HÓOHK'-ohl), luk'ul (LOOK'-ool); *salir; quitarse*
leave *tr. v.* hatzik (HAHTZ-eek), p'atik (P'AHT-eek); *dejarlo*
left *adj.* tz'ik (tz'eek); *izquierdo*
left hand *n.* tz'íih k'ab (TZ'ÉEE k'ahb); *mano izquierdo*
leftovers *n.* tz'ook (tz'oohk); *sobrante*
lend *tr. v.* maháantik (MAH-háahn-teek); *prestarlo*
length *n.* chowakil (CHOH-wahk-eel); *largura, longitud*
let *tr. v.* cha' (chah'); *permitir*

let's go! *imper.* ko'ox (koh'-ohsh); *¡vámanos! (vamos)*

letter *n.* hu'un (hoo'-oon); *carta*

lie *in. v.* tuus (tooos); *mentir*

lie down *in. v.* chiltal (CHEEL-tahl); *acostarse, echarse (en el suelo)*

lie (on the floor) *in. v.* chiltal (CHEEL-tahl); *echarse (en el suelo)*

lie (to someone) *tr. v.* tusik (TOOS-eek); *mentirle a uno*

life *in. v.* kuxtal (KOOSH-tahl); *viva*

light *n.* sáasil (SÁAHS-eel); *luz*

light *tr. v.* t'abik (T'AH-beek); *encenderlo, incendiarlo*

lightning *n.* u hatz'il cháak (oo HAHTZ'-eel CHÁAHK); *relámpago, rayo, rayo de cielo*

lightning bolt *n.* u hatz'il cháak (oo HAHTZ'-eel CHÁAHK); *rayo de cielo*

light (to become) *in. v.* sáastal (SÁAHS-tahl); *amanecer*

light (weight) *adj.* sáal (sáahl); *ligero, no pesado*

like (it, I) *adj.* utz tin wich (ootz teen WEECH); *me gusta*

like that *adv.* beyo' (BEH-yoh'); *así*

like this *adv.* beya' (BEH-yah'); *así*

lima bean *n.* iib (eeeb); *frijol lima, ibes*

lime (calcium carbonate, whitewash) *n.* ta'an (tah'-ahn); *cal*

lips *n.* bóox (bóohsh); *labios*

listen *tr. v.* u'uyik (OO'-OOY-eek); *escucharlo*

little *adj.* chan (chahn), mehen (MEH-hehn); ma' ya'abi' (MAH' yah'-ah-bee'); *pequeño, chico; no mucho, poco*

little (a) *adj.* chichan (CHEE-chahn); *poco*

little (a) *n.* hump'íit (HOOM-p'éeet); *un poco, pocos*

little by little *adv.* huhump'íitil (HOO-hoom-P'ÉEET-eel); *poco a poco*

live *in. v.* kaahtal (KAAH-tahl); *vivir*

liver *n.* táaman (TÁAHM-ahn); *hígado*

living *adj.* kuxa'an (KOO-shah'-ahn); *viviente*

lizard *n.* huuh (hoooh); *lagartija*

lizard (small) *n.* tóolok (TÓOH-lohk); *lagartija pequeña*

lizard (species of) *n.* meerech (MEEHR-ehch); *lagartija (una especie)*

load *n.* kuuch (koooch); *cargo*

loan *tr. v.* maháantik (MAH-háahn-teek); *prestarlo*

local *n. phr.* wayile' (wahy-EEL-eh'); *es de aquí*
locked *adj.* k'aalal (K'AAHL-ahl); *cerrado*
locust *n.* sáak' (sáahk'); *langosta de tierra, saltamontes*
long *adj.* chowak (CHOH-wahk); *largo*
long ago *adv.* úuchih (ÓOOCH-ee); *anteriormente*
look (at) *tr. v.* paktik (PAHK-teek); *mirarlo*
look at it! *imper.* pakteh (PAHK-teh); *¡mírelo!*
look for *tr. v.* kaxtik (KAHSH-teek); *buscarlo*
loosen *tr. v.* cha' (chah'), ch'ukik (CH'OOK-eek); *desatar*
lord *n.* yuum (yooom); *señor*
lose *tr. v.* satik (SAHT-eek); *perderlo*
lost *adj.* saatal (SAAH-tahl); *perdido*
lost (get) *in. v.* satpahal (saht-PAH-hahl); *desaparecerse*
lot (a) *adj.* ya'ab (yah'-ahb); *muchos*
loud *adj.* ch'e'eh (ch'eh'-eh); *bullicioso*
louse *n.* uk' (ook'); *piojo*
love *tr. v.* yaakuntik (yaah-KOON-teek); *amarlo*
low *adj.* kaabal (KAAHB-ahl); taam (taahm); *bajo; profundo, hondo*
lower *tr. v.* éensik (ÉEHN-seek); *bajarlo*
lying (on the ground) *adj.* pek'a'an (PEH-K'AH'-ahn); *tirado/hechado en el suelo*

M

macaw *n.* mo' (moh'); *guacamayo*
machete *n.* maskab (MAHS-kahb); *machete*
maiden *n.* suhuy pal (SOO-hooy pahl); *muchacha*
make *tr. v.* mentik (MEHN-teek); *hacerlo*
make (by hand) *tr. v.* mak'antik (MAH-k'ahn-TEEK); *hacerlo a mano*
make ready *tr. v.* li'sik (LEE'-seek); *alistarlo*
make tortillas *in. v.* pak'ach (PAHK'-ahch); *tortear*
make tortillas *tr. v.* pak'achtik (PAHK'-ahch-teek); *tortearlo*
male *n.* xiib (sheeeb); *varón, macho*
man *n.* máak (máahk); wíinik (WÉEEN-eek); xiib (sheeeb); yuum (yooom); *hombre; varón, macho*
man (lazy) *n.* hoykeep (HOHY-keehp); *hombre flojo*
man (old) *n.* nuxiib (NOO-sheeeb); nohoch wíinik (NOH-hoch WÉEEN-eek); *hombre viejo, anciano; viejo*

man's hairstyle *n.* xiibil tzo'otz (sheeeb-eel TZOH'-OHTZ); *pelo de macho*

many *adj.* ya'ab (yah'-ahb); ya'akach (YAH'-AH-kahch); *muchos*

many (there are) *adj.* ya'abo'ob (YAH'-AHB-oh'-ohb); *son muchos*

marijuana *n.* k'uutz (k'oootz); *marijuana*

marker stones *n.* xu'uk' (shoo'-ook'); *mojón*

married (to be) *in. v.* tz'oka'an beel (TZ'OHK-ah'-ahn beehl); *ser casado*

marrow *n.* tz'o'om (tz'oh'-ohm); *medula*

marry *in. v.* tz'o'okol beel (tz'oh'-OHK-ohl BEEHL); *casarse*

mash *in. v.* puch'ik (POOCH'-eek); *magullar*

masonry *n.* pak' (pahk'); *mampostería*

matter *n.* beel (beehl); *asunto*

mature *adj.* tak'an (TAH-k'ahn); *cocido; maduro*

mature *in. v.* tah (tah); *madurarse*

may *aux. v.* hu' chabale' (hoo' CHAHB-ahl-eh'); *se puede, se permite*

maybe *adv.* wale' (WAH-leh'); *tal vez, quizá*

may not *aux. v.* ma' u chabal (mah' oo CHAHB-ahl); *no se permite*

me *1st p. s. pron.* teen (teehn); *me*

meal *n.* hanal (HAHN-ahl), o'och (oh'-ohch); *comida*

measure *tr. v.* p'isik (P'EES-eek); *medirlo*

meat *n.* bak' (bahk'); *carne*

mecate (unit of land) *n.* p'isik'an (P'EES-eek'-ahn); *mecate*

medicine *n.* tz'aak (tz'aahk); *medicina*

medicine (for colds) *n.* tz'aak se'en (tz'aahk SEH'-ehn); *medicina para catarro*

metate *n.* ka'ah (kah'-ah); *metate*

Mexican (female) *n.* xwaach (eesh-WAAHCH); *mexicána*

Mexican (male) *n.* hwaach (ah-WAAHCH); *mexicáno*

middle *n.* chúumuk (CHÓOOM-ook); *centro, medio*

midnight *n.* chúumuk áak'ab (CHÓOOM-ook ÁAHK'-ahb); *media noche*

mill *n.* huch' (hooch'); *molino*

milpa (personal cornfield) *n.* kool (koohl); *milpa*

milpa tiller *n.* koolnáal (KOOHL-náahl); *milpero*

minor *n.* paal (paahl); *menor*

mirror *n.* néen (néehn); *espejo*
misfortune *n.* loob (loohb); *desgracia*
mist *n.* yeeb (yeehb); *neblina*
mix up *tr. v.* xa'ak'tik (SHAH'-AHK'-teek); *mezclarlo, revolverlo*
moist *adj.* ch'uul (ch'oool); *mojado*
moisten *tr. v.* ch'ulik (CH'OOL-eek); *mojarlo*
money *n.* taak'in (TAAH-k'een); *dinero*
monkey *n.* tuucha (TOOOCH-ah); *mono*
monkey (general) *n.* ma'ax (mah'-ahsh); *mono*
monkey (howler) *n.* baatz' (baahtz'); *mono aullador, saraguate*
monkey (spider) *n.* chuwen (CHOO-wehn); *mono, saraguate*
morning *adv.* hatzkab k'iin (hahtz-kahb K'EEEN); *la mañana*
mosquito *n.* k'oxol (K'OHSH-ohl); *mosquito, mosco*
mother *n.* nah' (nah'); *madre*
mouse *n.* ch'o' (ch'oh'); *ratón*
moustache *n.* me'ex (meh'-ehsh); *bigote*
mouth *n.* chi' (chee'); *boca*
move *in. v.* péek (péehk); *moverse*
move *tr. v.* péeksik (PÉEHK-seek); *moverlo*
movement *n.* péek (péehk); *movimiento*
much *adj.* hach ya'ab (hahch YAH'-ahb); ya'ab (yah'-ahb); *mucho; muchos*
much (not) *adj.* ma' ya'abi' (mah' YAH'-AHB-ee'); *no mucho*
mucus *n.* síim (séeem); *moco*
muddy *adj.* puuk (poook); *turbio*
muggy *adj.* k'as k'íilkab (k'ahs K'ÉEEL-kahb); *medio sudando, húmedo*
music *n.* k'aay (k'aahy); *música*
mute person *n.* htoot (ah-TOOHT); *persona muda*

N

naked *adj.* chaknul (chahk-NOOL); xma' nook' (EESH-mah' nook'); *desnudo*
name *n.* k'aba' (K'AH-bah'); *nombre*
napkin *adj.* háay (háahy); *servilleta*
narrow *adj.* kóom (kóohm); *estrecho*

native *n. phr.* wayile' (wahy-EEL-eh'); *es de aquí*

near *adj.* naatz' (naahtz'); *cerca*

necessary *adj.* k'abéet (K'AHB-éeht), k'a'ana'an (K'AH'-AH-nah'-ahn); *necesario*

necessity *n.* nu'kul (NOO'K-ool); *necesidad*

neck *n.* kaal (kaahl); *cuello*

needle *n.* púutz' (póootz'); *aguja*

nerve *n.* xiich' (sheeech'); *nervio*

nest *n.* k'u' (k'oo'); *nido*

nettle *n.* láal (láahl); *ortiga, chichicasta*

never *adv.* ma'a tech (MAH'-AH tehch); mix bik'in (meesh BEE-k'een); *jamás; nunca*

new *adj.* túumben (TÓOOM-behn); *nuevo*

nice *adj.* hatz'utz (HAHTZ'-ootz); ki' (kee'); lukum (LOO-koom); *hermoso, bonito, bello; bueno*

nice (very) *adj.* sen utz (SEHN ootz); *buenísimo, muy bien*

night *n.* ak'ab (AHK'-ahb); *noche*

night (to become) *in. v.* áak'abtal (áahk'-AHB-tahl); *anocher*

nightmare *n.* k'aas wayak' (k'aahs WAHY-ahk'); *mal sueño, pesadilla*

nine *n.* bolon (BOH-lohn) (hypothetical); *nueve*

no *adv.* ma' (mah'); *no*

noise *n.* huum (hooom); *ruido*

noisy *adj.* ch'e'eh (ch'eh'-eh); *ruidoso, bullicioso*

noon *n.* chúumuk k'iin (CHÓOOM-ook K'EEEN); *media día*

no one *pron.* mix máak (MEESH máahk); *ninguno, nadie*

north *n.* xaman (SHAH-mahn); *norte*

north wind *n.* xaman ka'an (shah-mahn KAH'-AHN); *cierzo, viento del norte*

nose *n.* ni' (nee'); *nariz*

not *adv.* ma' (mah'); *no*

nothing *pron.* mix ba'al (meesh BAH'-ahl); *nada*

notice *tr. v.* ohéeltik (oh-HÉEHL-teek); *notar*

not me *adv.* ma' teeni' (mah' TEEHN-ee'); *yo no*

not much *adj.* ma' ya'abi' (MAH' yah'-ah-bee'); *no mucho, poco*

not possible *adj.* mix táan u beeta'ale' (meesh TÁAHN oo beeh-tah'-AHL-eh'); *no es posible*

nourish *tr. v.* tzeentik (TZEEHN-teek); *darle la comida, criar*

nowadays *n.* behla'(e') (beh-LAH'-[eh']); *hoy*
nowhere *n.* mix tu'ux (MEESH too'-oosh); *en ninguna parte*

O

obligation *n.* kuuch (koooch); *obligación, carga*
odor *n.* ch'e'eh (CH'EH'-eh), book (boohk); *olor*
offer *tr. v.* wak (wahk); *ofrecer*
offered *tr. v.* wa'ak (wah'-ahk); *ofrecido*
OK *adj.* ma'alob (mah'-AHL-ohb); *bien*
old *adj.* ch'iha'an (CH'EE-hah'-ahn); nohoch (NOH-hoch); nuxib (NOOH-sheeb); úuchben (ÓOOCH-behn); *viejo; anciano; antiguo*
old man *n.* nohoch wíinik (NOH-hoch WÉEEN-eek), nuxiib (NOOH-sheeeb); *viejo, anciano*
old (to make) *in. v.* ch'iih (ch'eeeh); *hacer viejo*
old woman *n.* nohoch ko'olel (NOH-hoch koh'-ohl-EHL), xnuuk (eesh-NOOOK); *vieja*
omen *n.* tamax chi' (TAH-mahsh CHEE'); *agüero*
on *prep.* ti' (tee'); *en*
one *n.* hun (hoon); *uno*
one hundred *n.* ho' k'áal (HOH' k'áahl) (hypothetical); *cien, ciento*
one (inanimate thing) *adj., pron.* hump'éel (hoom-P'ÉEHL); *un(a) (cosa)*
one (long thing) *adj., pron.* huntz'íit (hoon-TZ'ÉEET); *un(a) (cosa larga)*
one (person or animal, animate thing) *adj., pron.* huntúul (hoon-TÓOOL); *un(a) (persona o animal)*
one (tree) *adj., pron.* hunkúul (hoon-KÓOOL); *un(a) (árbol)*
open *in. v.* heeb (heehb); *abrirse*
open *tr. v.* hebik (heh-BEEK); *abrirlo*
opened *adj.* heban/he'an/he'ik (heh-BAHN/heh'-AHN/heh'-EEK); *abierto*
opening *n.* chi' (chee'); hool (hoohl); *boca; hoyo, hueco*
or *inter.* wáah (wáah); *o*
orange juice *n.* k'aab china (k'aahb CHEE-nah); *jugo de naranja*
orange (sour) *n.* chiinah pah (CHEEE-nah PAH); *naranja agria*

orange (sweet) *n.* chiinah (CHEEE-nah); *naranja dulce*
orange (tree, sour) *n.* pak'áal (PAHK'-áahl); *naranjo*
order *tr. v.* tusbeltik (toos-BEHL-teek); *mandarlo, ordenarlo*
order (put in) *tr. v.* tzolik (TZOHL-eek); *ordenarlo*
origin *n.* chuun (chooon); *origen, raíz, principio*
oriole *n.* k'ubul (K'OOB-ool); *oriol*
other *adj.* láak' (láahk'); heel (heehl); *otro*
overcast *adj.* nóokoy (NÓOHK-ohy); *nublado*
overcast (to become) *in. v.* nóokoytal (NÓOHK-ohy-tahl); *nublarse*
overtake *tr. v.* chukpachtik (chook-PAHCH-teek); *alcanzar*
owl *n.* buuh (booo); tunkuluchú (toon-koo-loo-CHOO); *ecolote, búho*
owner *n.* yuum (yooom); *dueño*
ox *n.* wakax (WAHK-ahsh); *buey*

P

paca (rodent, spotted cavy, *Cuniculus paca*) *n.* haaleb (HAAHL-ehb); *tapescuintle*
pack *tr. v.* but'ik (BOOT'-eek); *embutirlo*
pain *n.* k'i'inam (K'EE'-EE'-nahm), yaah (yaah); *dolor*
pain (general expression of) *dem.* ay (ahy); *¡ay, dios!*
painful *adj.* yah (yah); *doloroso*
paint *n.* bon (bohn); *pintura*
paint *tr. v.* bonik (BOHN-eek); *pintarlo*
painted *adj.* boonol/bo'on (BOOHN-ohl/boh'-ohn); *pintado*
pale *adj.* poos (poohs); *descolorido, palido, desteñido*
palm thatch *n.* xa'an (shah'-ahn); *palmo para techo, guano*
pants *n.* eex (eehsh); *pantalon*
papaya *n.* puut (pooot); *papaya*
paper *n.* hu'un (hoo'-oon); *papel*
parent *n.* láak (láahk); *pariente*
parrot *n.* xt'uut' (eesh-T'OOOT'); *loro, perico*
pass *tr. v.* mansik (MAHN-seek); *pasarlo*
pass by *in. v.* máan (máahn); *pasar*
pass through *tr. v.* potik (POHT-eek); *transpasarlo*
pay (for) *tr. v.* bo'otik (BOH'-OHT-eek); *pagarlo*

peccary (collared) (javalina, *Pecari tajacu*) *n.* kitam (KEE-tam); *jabalí, coche del monte*

penetrate *tr. v.* potik (POHT-eek); *penetrarlo*

penis *n.* toon (toohn); xiibil (sheeeb-eel); *pene, picha*

pepper *n.* iik (eeek); *chile, ají*

perceive *tr. v.* u'uyik (OO'-OOY-eek); *percibirlo*

perhaps *adv.* wale' (WAH-leh'); *tal vez, quizá*

perhaps (it is so) *adv.* beey wale' (beehy WAHL-eh'); *¡tal vez es posible!*

permit *tr. v.* cha(ik) (CHAH-[eek]); *permitirlo, dejarlo*

person *n.* máak (máahk); wíinik (WÉEEN-eek); *persona*

perspiration *adj.* k'íilkab (K'ÉEEL-kahb); *sudor*

pet *n.* aalak' (AAHL-ahk'); *animal doméstico, mascota*

physician (female) *n.* xtz'aak (eesh-TZ'AAHK); *doctora, médica*

physician (male) *n.* htz'aak (ah-TZ'AAHK); *doctor, médico*

piece *n.* xéet' (shéeht'); *pedazo*

piece (continuous) *n.* baab (baahb); *pedazo (continuo)*

pig *n.* aak (aahk); k'éek'en (K'ÉEH-k'ehn); *puerco*

pillar *n.* okom (OHK-ohm); *pilar, horcón*

pillow (folded cloth used as) *n.* xk'áanho'ol (eesh-K'ÁAHN-hoh'-ohl); *almohada*

pink *adj.* chakpose'en (chahk-poh-SEH'-ehn); *rosada*

pit (for cooking) *n.* píib (péeeb); *barbacoa, horno*

place *n.* baanda (BAAHND-ah); kaah (kaah), kaahtal (KAAH-tahl); *parte; lugar*

place *tr. v.* tz'íik (tz'éeek); *ponerlo*

plant *n.* pak'al (PAHK'-ahl); *planta*

plant *in. v.* pak'al (PAHK'-ahl); *plantar, sembrar*

plant *tr. v.* pak'ik (PAHK'-eek); *sembrarlo*

play *in. v.* báaxal (BÁASH-ahl); *jugar*

play *tr. v.* báaxtik (BÁASH-teek); *jugarlo*

plum (wild) *n.* abal (AHB-ahl); *ciruela*

point *n.* u yeh (oo yeh); *punto*

pole *n.* che' (cheh'); *palo, vara*

polish *tr. v.* yúultik (YÓOOL-teek); *bruñirlo*

poor *adj.* óotzil (ÓOHTZ-eel); *pobre*

Pope *n.* papah (PAH-pah); *el Papa*

porcupine *n.* k'i'ix pech ooch (K'EE'-EESH pehch OOHCH); *cuerpo espín*

pork (baked, roasted) *n.* pibil k'éek'en (PEEB-eel k'éeh-k'ehn); *conchinita pibil*

portion *n.* xéet' (shéeht'); *pedazo*

posol (corn gruel) *n.* k'eyem (K'EH-yehm); *pozole*

possible *adv.* beytz'abile' (BEHY-tz'ahb-EEL-eh'); *posible*

possible (if) *adj.* he' u beeta'ale' (heh' oo BEEH-tah'-ahl-eh'); *si se puede*

possible (it is) *adj.* hu' u biita'ale' (hooh' oo BEEE-tah'-AHL-eh'); *es posible*

possible (not) *adj.* mix táan u beeta'ale' (meesh TÁAHN oo BEEH-tah'-AHL-eh'); *no es posible*

possibly *adj., prep.* le ka'a p'éelil (leh kah'-ah P'ÉEH-leel); *posible*

post *n.* okom (OHK-ohm); *poste*

pound *tr. v.* pak'achtik (pahk'-AHCH-teek); *machacarlo*

pregnant *adj.* yo'om (yoh'-ohm); *embarazada*

pregnant (to become) *in. v.* yo'omchahtal (yoh'-ohm-CHAH-tahl); *embarazarse*

prepare *tr. v.* li'sik (LEE'-seek); mak'antik (mah-K'AHN-teek); *prepararlo*

present *n.* síihbil (SÉEEB-eel); *regalo*

pretty *adj.* ki'ichpam (KEE'-EECH-pahm); *bonito*

previously *adv.* ka'ach (kah'-ahch); *antiguamente, entonces*

price *n.* tohol (TOH-hohl); *precio*

prickly pear cactus *n.* páak'am (PÁAHK'-ahm); *nopal, tuna*

prior *prep.* yáax (yáahsh); *previo*

problem *n.* ba'te'el (BAH'-teh'-ehl); *pelea, problema*

prognostication *n.* tamax chi' (TAH-mahsh CHEE'); *agüero*

protect *tr. v.* ta'akik (TAH'-AHK-eek); *cuidarlo, guardarlo*

pull *tr. v.* kóolik (KÓOHL-eek); páaytik (PÁAHY-teek); *jalarlo*

puma *n.* koh (koh); *puma*

pumpkin *n.* k'úum (k'óoom); *calabaza*

pumpkin seeds *n.* sikil (SEEK-eel); *pepita de calabaza*

punch (with fist) *tr. v.* loxik (LOHSH-eek); *pegarlo con puño cerado*

pursue *tr. v.* chukpachtik (chook-PAHCH-teek); *alcanzar al que va adelante*

pus *n.* puh (poo); *pus, materia de llaga*

put *tr. v.* tz'íik (tz'éeek); *ponerlo*

put in order *tr. v.* tzolik (TZOHL-eek); *ordenarlo*
put on (clothes) *tr. v.* búukintik (bóoo-KEEN-teek); *vestirse, ponerlo ropa*
put out (fire, light) *tr. v.* tupik (TOO-peek); *apagarlo*
pyramid *n.* muul (moool); *pirámide*

Q

quail *n.* beech' (beehch'); *codorniz*
queer (homosexual) *n.* xch'úupul xib (eesh-CH'ÓOOP-ool SHEEB); *maricón* (derogatory), *waco*
quern and grindstone *n.* k'abka' (K'AHB-kah'); *metate y mano*
quick *adj.* séebak (SÉEHB-ahk); *rápido*
quickly *adv.* séeb (séehb); *rápido*

R

rabbit *n.* t'u'ul (T'OO'-ool); *conejo*
raccoon *n.* k'ulu' (K'OOL-oo'); *mapache*
rain *n.* cháak (cháahk), ha' (hah'); *lluvia*
raise *tr. v.* li'isik (LEE'-EES-eek); *levantarlo*
ranch *n.* kaahtal (KAAH-tahl); *rancho*
rapidly (work) *adj.* áalkab meyah (ÁAHL-kahb MEHY-ah); *trabajar muy rápido*
rat *n.* ch'o' (ch'oh'); *rata*
rather *adv.* sam (sahm); *apenas*
rattlesnake *n.* tzáa'kaan (tzáah'-KAAHN); *culebra tipo de cascabel*
read *tr. v.* xook (shoohk); xokik (SHOHK-eek); *leer; contarlo*
ready (oneself) *refl. v.* li'isik u ba (LEE'-EES-eek oo BAH); *prepararse*
ready (make) *tr. v.* li'sik (LEE'-seek); *alistarlo*
rear *tr. v.* tzeentik (TZEEHN-teek); *criar*
reason *n.* nu'ukul (NOO'-OOK-ool), tuukul (TOOOK-ool); *razón*
receive *tr. v.* k'amik (K'AHM-eek); *recibir*
recognize *tr. v.* k'ahóoltik (K'AH-óohl-TEEK); *reconocerlo*
recount *tr. v.* tzikbatik (TZEEK-bah-TEEK); *recontarlo*
red *adj.* chak (chahk); *colorado, rojo*

red food dye (annatto) *n.* k'iwi' (K'EE-wee'); k'uxu' (K'OO-shoo'); *achiote*

redheaded *adj.* ch'eel (ch'eehl); *rubio*

redheaded child *n.* chan ch'eel (CHAHN ch'eehl); *niño güero*

reed *n.* siit (seeet); *popote*

relative *n.* láak' (láahk'), chilankabil (chee-lahn-KAHB-eel); *miembro de familia, pariente*

release *tr. v.* cha' (chah'); *soltar*

remain *in. v.* p'áatal (P'ÁAH-tahl); *quedarse*

repair *tr. v.* utzkíintik (ootz-KÉEEN-teek); *repararlo*

reprimand *tr. v.* k'eyik (K'EHY-eek); *reprenderlo, reñirlo*

reservoir *n.* aak'al (AAHK'-ahl); *embalse*

reside *in. v.* kaahtal (KAAH-tahl); *vivir*

resin *n.* iitz (eeetz); *resina o leche de árbol*

rest *in. v.* he'elel (heh'-ehl-EHL); *descansar*

rest oneself *refl. v.* he'esik u ba (HEH'-EHS-eek oo bah); *descansarse*

return *in. v.* suut (sooot); *regresar*

return *tr. v.* sutik (SOO-teek); *devolverlo*

returned (to be) *in. v.* su'utal (SOO'-OO-tahl); *devolver*

rich *adj.* ayik'al (ahy-EEK'-ahl), taak'inal (TAAH-k'een-ahl); *rico*

right away *adv.* naapulak (naah-POOL-ahk); *en seguido*

right here *adv.* te'ela' (TEH'-EH-lah'); *allí*

right side *n.* no'oh (noh'-oh); *lado derecho*

right there *adv.* te'elo' (TEH'-EH-loh'); *allá*

right (to the) *n. phr.* (ti') no'oh ([tee'] NOH'-oh); *a la derecha*

ripe *adj.* k'an (k'ahn), tak'an (TAH-k'ahn); *maduro*

ripe (for the picking) *adj.* yi'h (yee'h); *sazonado*

ripen *in. v.* tah (tah); *madurarse, sazonarse*

ripen *tr. v.* yi'htal (YEE'H-tahl); *sazonarse*

rise *in. v.* líik'il (LÉEEK'-eel); *levantarse*

road *n.* beel (beehl); *camino*

roast *tr. v.* k'a'atik (K'AH'-AH-teek); *asarlo*

roasted *adj.* k'a'bil (K'AH'-beel), pokbil (POHK-beel); *asado*

rock *n.* tuunich (TOOON-eech); *piedra*

roll *tr. v.* kopik (KOH-peek); *enrollar*

roll up *tr. v.* to'ik (TOH'-eek); *enrollarlo*

roof *n.* u ho'ol nah (oo HOH'-OHL nah), u pool nah (oo POOHL nah); *techo*

rooster *n.* t'eel (t'eehl); *gallo*

root *n.* mootz (moohtz); *raíz*

rope *n.* suum (sooom); *soga*

rose *n.* lool (loohl); *rosa*

round *adj.* wolis (WOHL-ees); *redondo*

rub *tr. v.* yúultik (YÓOOL-teek); *frotarlo*

rump *n.* bak'el iit (BAHK'-ehl EEET), p'u'ukil iit (P'OO'-OOK-eel EEET); *nalga*

run *in. v.* áalkab (ÁAHL-kahb); *correr*

rust *n.* itz (eetz); *oxidado*

S

sack *n.* sáabukaan (SÁAH-boo-kaahn); *bolsa, morral*

saddle quern *n.* ka'ah (kah'-ah); *metate*

saints *pl. n.* k'uho'ob (K'OO-hoh'-ohb); *santos*

salesman *n.* koonol (KOOHN-ohl); *vendedor*

saleswoman *n.* xkoonol (eesh-KOOHN-ohl); *vendedora*

salt *n.* ta'ab (tah'-ahb); *sal*

salt *tr. v.* ta'abik (TAH'-AHB-eek); *salar*

same *aux. v.* éet (éeht); *mismo*

sandal *n.* xanab (SHAH-nahb); *guarache*

sap *n.* iitz (eeetz); *resina o leche de árbol*

sapote *n.* ya' (yah'); *zapote*

say *tr. v.* a'alik (AH'-AHL-[eek]); t'anik (T'AHN-eek); *decirlo; hablarlo, llamarlo*

scare *tr. v.* p'u'uhsik (P'OO'-OO-seek), sahahkúuns (SAH-hah-kóoons); *espantarlo*

scold *tr. v.* k'eyik (K'EHY-eek); *regañarlo*

scoop up (excrement) *tr. v.* pitik (PEE-teek); *sacar excremento con cuchara*

scorpion *n.* síina'an (séee-NAH'-AHN); *escorpion*

scram! *imper.* xeen te'elo' (sheehn-TEH'-EH-loh'); *¡váyate!*

scram! (to pigs, chickens, etc.) *imper.* huchi (HOOCH-ee); *¡vete! (a puercos, pollos, etc.)*

scrambled *adj.* puuk' (poook'); *revueltos*

scrape *tr. v.* páanik (PÁAHN-eek); *cavarlo*

screw *tr. v.* kopik (KOH-peek); *atornillar*

seated *adj.* hetz'a'an (HEHTZ'-ah'-ahn), kula'an (koo-LAH'-ahn); *sentado,*

secondhand *adj.* asben/asbe'en (AHS-behn/ AHS-beh'-ehn); *de medio uso*

secured *adj.* hetz'a'an (HEHTZ'-ah'-ahn); *asegurado*

see *tr. v.* ilik (EEL-eek); *verlo*

seed *n.* i'inah (EE'-EE-nah); neek' (neehk'); *semilla para sembrar maíz; semilla, pepita*

seedbed (raised) *n.* ka'anche' (KAH'-AHN-che'); *plantío elevado*

seeder (stick for planting) *n.* xúul (shóool); *coa, sembrador*

seeds (pumpkin/squash) *n.* sikil (SEEK-eel); *pepita de calabaza*

see it! *imper.* ileh (EEL-eh); *¡vélo!*

seek *tr. v.* kaxtik (KAHSH-teek); *buscarlo*

seize *tr. v.* ch'aik (CH'AH-eek); *agarrarlo, llevarlo*

sell *tr. v.* konik (KOHN-eek); *venderlo*

send *tr. v.* túuxtik (TÓOOSH-teek); *enviarlo*

settled *adj.* hetz'a'an (HEHTZ'-ah'-ahn); *firme, asentado, fundado*

seven *n.* uk (ook) (hypothetical); *siete*

sew *in. v.* chuuy (choooy); *costurar*

shade *n.* bo'oy (BOH'-ohy); *sombra*

shadow *n.* bo'oy (BOH'-ohy); *sombra*

shake *in. v.* tíit (téeet); *sacudirse*

shake *tr. v.* péeksik (PÉEHK-seek), tíitik (TÉEET-eek); *sacudirlo*

shaman *n.* hmeen (ah-MEEN); *curandero*

shame *n.* su'utal (SOO'-OO-tahl); *vergüenza*

share *tr. v.* t'oxik (T'OHSH-eek); *repartirlo, distribuirlo*

sharpness *adj.* paapil (PAAHP-eel); *picante*

shave *tr. v.* tz'ikik (TZ'EEK-eek); *afeitarlo*

shaven *adj.* tz'ika'an (tz'ee-KAH'-ahn); *afeitado*

shawl *n.* booch' (boohch'); *rebozo*

sheep *n.* htaman (ah-TAH-mahn); *borrego*

shell *n.* sóol (sóohl); *cáscara*

shell corn *tr. v.* oxo'ontik (OHSH-oh'-ohn-TEEK); *desgranarlo*

shoe *n.* xanab (SHAH-nahb); *zapato*

shoot *tr. v.* tz'onik (TZ'OHN-eek); *dispararlo, tirarlo*

short *adj.* koom (koohm); *corto*

shotgun *n.* tz'oon (tz'oohn); *escopeta*

shoulder *n.* kelembal (KEH-lehm-bahl); *hombro*

shout *n.* awat (AH-waht); *grito*

show *n.* cha'an (chah'-ahn); *espectáculo*

show *tr. v.* e'esik (EH'-EHS-eek), tzikbatik (tzeek-bah-TEEK); *mostrarlo*

show oneself *refl. v.* e'esk u bah (EH'-EHSK oo BAH); *mostrarse*

sibling (true) *n.* láak'tzil (LÁAHK'-tzeel); *hermano(a) verdadero(a)*

sick *adj.* k'oha'an (K'OH-hah'-ahn); *enfermo*

side *n.* háal (háahl); tzéel (tzéehl); *orilla; lado*

signal (by hand) *in. v.* payk'ab (PAHY-k'ahb); *señalar; señal*

sin *n.* k'eban (K'EH-bahn), siip/si'ip(il) (SEEEP/SEE'-EEP-[eel]); *pecado*

sinew *n.* xiich' (sheeech'); *tendón*

sing *in. v.* k'aay (k'aahy); *cantar*

single *adj.* hun (hoon); *solito, solo*

sink *tr. v.* t'ubik (t'oob-EEK); *hundirlo*

sinkhole *n.* tz'ono'ot (TZ'OH-noh'-oht); *cenote*

sister (older) *n.* kiik (keeek); *hermana mayor*

sister (true sibling) *n.* láak'tzil (LÁAHK'-tzeel); *hermana verdadera*

sister (younger) *n.* íitz'in (ÉEETZ'-een); *hermana*

sister (youngest) *n.* xt'uup (eesh-T'OOOP); last female child in family; *hermana menor; última niña de la familia*

sit *in. v.* kulal (KOOH-lahl); *sentar*

sit down *in. v.* kultal (KOOL-tahl); *sentarse*

six *n.* wak (wahk) (hypothetical); *seis*

sixty *n.* óox k'áal (ÓOHSH k'aahl) (hypothetical); *sesenta*

size *n.* nohochil (noh-hoh-CHEEL); *tamaño*

skin *n.* k'éewel (K'ÉEH-wehl); *piel*

skinny *adj.* tz'oya'an (tz'oy-AH'-AHN); *flaco*

skunk *n.* páayooch (PÁAHY-oohch); *zorillo*

sky *n.* ka'an (kah'-ahn); *cielo*

slab (of stone) *n.* hayam (HAHY-ahm); *laja*

sleep *in. v.* wenel (WEHN-ehl); *dormir*

slender *adj.* bek'ech (BEH-k'ehch); *delgado*

slice *tr. v.* tah (tah); *rabanar*

sliced *adj.* taahal (TAAH-hahl); *rabinado*

slightly *adv.* sam (sahm); *un poco*

slippery *adj.* hahalkil (hah-hahl-KEEL); *liso, resbaloso*

slope *n.* níix (néeesh); *cuesta, ladera, inclinación*

slow *adj.* chaanbeel (CHAAHN-beehl); *despacio, lento*

small *adj.* chan (chahn), chichan (CHEE-chahn), mehen (MEH-hen); *pequeño, chico*

smallest part *n.* t'uup (t'ooop); *parte más pequeño, el menor*

smash *tr. v.* petz'ik (PEHTZ'-eek); *destrozar*

smell *n.* bok (bohk); *olor*

smell *tr. v.* u'yik (OO'-yeek); *olerlo, sentir olor*

smoke *n.* buutz' (boootz'); *humo*

smoke *in. v.* tz'u'utz' (TZ'OO'-ootz');*fumar*

smoke *tr. v.* tz'u'utz'ik (TZ'OO'-ootz'-EEK);*fumarlo*

smooth *adj.* hoholkil (hoh-hohl-KEEL); táax (táahsh); *liso; llano, plano*

snail (land) *n.* úurich (ÓOOR-eech); *caracol de tierra*

snake *n.* kaan (kaahn); *culebra*

snare *n.* peetz' (peehtz'); *trampa*

soil *n.* lu'um (loo'-oom); *tierra*

soldier *n.* waach (waahch); *soldado*

someone *n.* wáah máax (wáah MÁAHSH); *alguien*

something *n.* wáah ba'ax (wáah BAH'-ahsh); *algo*

somewhat *n.* k'aas (k'aahs); *de una parte, un poquito*

somewhere *n.* wáah tu'ux (wáah TOO'-oosh); *algún lugar*

son *n.* paal (paahl); *hijo*

song *n.* k'aay (k'aahy); *canción*

soon *adv.* ka'aka't(e') (KAH'-AH-kah'-t[e']); *al rato, un poco después, más tarde*

soot *n.* sabak (SAH-bahk); *tizne*

soul *n.* pixaan (PEESH-aahn); *alma*

sound *n.* huum (hooom); *sonido*

sour *adj.* pah (pah); *agrio*

source *n.* sayab (SAHY-ahb);*fuente, ojo de agua*

sour orange *n.* pak'áal (PAHK'-áahl); *naranja agria*

sour orange (tree) *n.* pak'áal (PAHK'-áahl); *naranjo agrio*

soursop (custard apple) *n.* óop (óohp); *anona*

south *n.* nohol (NOH-hohl); *sur*

sow *in. v.* pak'al (PAHK'-ahl); *sembrar*

sow *tr. v.* pak'ik (PAHK'-eek); *sembrarlo*

sown *par.* pak'a'an (PAHK'-ah'-ahn); *sembrado*

spark *n.* xikin k'aak' (shee-keen K'AAHK'); *chispa*

speak *in. v.* t'aan (t'aahn); *hablar, decir*

spectacle *n.* cha'an (chah'-ahn); *espectáculo*

speech *n.* t'aan (t'aahn); *idioma, lengua*

spicy *adj.* páap (páahp); *picante*

spider *n.* am (ahm); *araña*

spill *tr. v.* wekik (WEH-keek); *derremarlo*

spilled *adj.* weehel/weekel (WEEH-hehl/WEEH-kehl); *derramado*

spill (water) *tr. v.* wekik ha' (WEH-keek HAH');
derramar agua

spindle *n.* pechéech (PEH-chéehch); *huso*

spine *n.* t'o'ol (t'oh'-ohl); *espinazo*

spirit *n.* ik' (eek'), óol (oohl), pixaan (PEESH-aahn);
espíritu

spirit substitute *n.* wáayhéel (WÁAHY-héehl); *nahual,*
espíritu

split *adj.* kaacha'al (kaah-CHAH'-ahl); *hendido*

split (long things) *tr. v.* kachik (KAH-cheek); *hender*
(cosas largas)

spouse *n.* láak' (láahk'); *esposo*

spring *n.* aak'al (AAHK'-ahl), sayab (SAHY-ahb), sayap
ha' (SAHY-ahp HAH'); *ciénega, ojo de agua*

spur *n.* aach (aahch); *espuela*

spy *tr. v.* ch'úuk (CH'ÓOOK); *espiar*

squash *n.* k'úum (k'óoom); *calabaza*

squash seeds *n.* sikil (SEEK-eel); *pepita de calabaza*

squirrel *n.* ku'uk (KOO'-ook); *ardilla*

stand *refl. v.* wa'ak u ba (WAH'-AHK oo bah); *pararse*

stand up! *imper.* wa'altal (WAH'-AHL-tahl); *¡pongase*
de pie!

stand up *in. v.* wa'al (wah'-ahl); *pararse, ponerse de pie*

star *n.* eek' (eehk'); *estrella*

start (a fight) *tr. v.* ketik (KEH-teek); *empezar una pelea*

started (to get) *in. v.* chunpahal (choon-PAH-hahl);
empezarse, comenzar

stay *in. v.* p'áatal (P'ÁAH-tahl); *quedarse*

stay here *imper.* p'aten waye' (P'AH-tehn WAH-yeh');
quédase aquí

steal *in. v.* ookol (OOHK-ohl); *hurtar, robar*

steal *tr. v.* oklik (OHK-leek); *hurtarlo, robarlo*

stem *n.* chun (choon); *raíz, principio, tronco*

stepfather *n.* mahan yuum (MAH-hahn YOOOM);
padrastro

stew *n.* k'óol (k'óohl); *guiso*

stick *n.* che' (cheh'); *palo, vara*

stick around *in. v.* xáantal (SHÁAHN-tahl); *tardarse*

stick (for digging) *n.* lóob (lóohb); *coa*

stick (for planting) *n.* xúul (shóool); *coa, sembrador*

stiff *adj.* t'iinil (T'EEEN-eel); *tieso*

still (not moving) *adj.* wa'bal (WAH'-bahl); *inmóvil*

sting *n.* aach (aahch); *picadura*

stocked (well-) *adj.* babahkil (BAHB-ah-keel);
bien surtido

stolen *adj.* ookolbil (OOHK-ohl-BEEL); *robado, hurtado*

stomach *n.* nak' (nahk'); *estómago, barriga, panza*

stone *n.* tuunich (TOOON-eech); *piedra*

stone (crushed limestone) *n.* sahkab (SAH-kahb),
saskab (SAHS-kahb); *roca calcárea deleznable,
sascab*

stone (hard) *n.* tok' tuunich (tohk' TOOON-eech);
pedernal, piedra dura

stone house *n.* pak'il nah (pahk'-eel NAH); *casa
de piedra*

stones (for marking land) *pl. n.* xu'uk' (SHOO'-ook');
mojónes

stool *n.* k'anche' (K'AHN-cheh'); *banqueta para sentarse*

stop! *imper.* wa'alen (WAH'-AHL-ehn); *¡alto!, ¡párate!*

stop *in. v.* wa'al (wah'-ahl); *pararse*

stopped *adj.* wa'bal (WAH'-bahl); *parado*

storm *n.* chichiik' (CHEECH-eeek'); *tempestad,
temporal, huracán*

straight *adj.* toh (toh); *derecho, recto, directo*

strange *adj.* hela'an (HEH-lah'-ahn); *extraño*

stranger *n.* tz'uul (tz'oool); *extranjero, ladino*

stranger (female) *n.* xunáan (SHOO-náahn);
extranjera, ladina

strap *n.* k'axab nak' (k'ahsh-AHB nahk'); *faja*

straw *n.* siit (seeet); *popote*

straw hat *n.* xa'anil p'ook (SHAH'-AHN-eel P'OOHK);
sombrero de paja

strength *n.* muuk' (moook'); *fuerza*

stretch *tr. v.* satz'ik (SAHTZ'-eek); *estirarlo*

strike *tr. v.* hatz'ik (HAHTZ'-eek); *golpearlo, pegarlo*

strong *adj.* chich (cheech); k'a'am (K'AH'-ahm);
fuerte; recio

study *tr. v.* xokik (SHOHK-eek); *contarlo*

stuff *tr. v.* but'ik (BOOT'-eek); *llenarlo*

stupid *adj.* nuum (nooom), tz'u'uy pool (TZ'OO'-OOY
poohl); *estúpido, tonto*

submerge *tr. v.* t'ubik (T'OOB-eek); *sumirlo*

submerged *adj.* t'uubul/t'ubukbal (T'OOO-bool/T'OO-
book-bahl); *hundido, sumido*

substitute *tr. v.* k'exik (K'EHSH-eek); *trocarlo*

substituted *adj.* k'eexel (K'EEHSH-ehl); *trocado*

suck *in. v.* tz'u'utz' (tz'oo'-ootz'); *chupar*

suck *tr. v.* tz'u'utz'ik (tz'oo'-ootz'-EEK); *chuparlo*

sugar *n.* asukaar (ah-SOO-kaahr); Sp. loanword; *azúcar*

sun *n.* k'iin (k'eeen); *sol*

sunken *adj.* t'uubul/t'ubukbal (T'OOO-bool/ T'OO-book-bahl); *hundido, sumido*

sunset *n.* bin ka ak'abtal (been kah ahk'-AHB-tahl); *anochecer*

super *adj.* sen ma'alob (sehn MAH'-AHL-ohb); *buenísimo*

support *tr. v.* tzeentik (TZEEHN-teek); *mantener, apoyar*

sure (to be) *adv.* he'ele' (HEH'-EHL-eh'); *sí, claro*

surprising *adj.* hak'óolal (hahk'-ÓOHL-ahl); *sorprendent*

suspend *tr. v.* ch'uytal (CH'OOY-tahl); *colgarlo*

suspended (to be) *refl. v.* ch'uyul (CH'OOY-ool); *suspenderse*

swallow *in. v.* luuk' (loook'); *tragar*

swamp *n.* aak'al (AAHK'-ahl); *pantano*

sweep *tr. v.* míistik (MÉEES-teek); *barrerlo*

sweepings *n.* u ta' míis (oo tah' MÉEES); *basura barrida*

sweet *adj.* ch'uhuk (CH'OO-hook); *dulce*

sweet potato *n.* iis (eees); *camote*

swim *in. v.* báab (báahb); *nadar*

swollen *adj.* chuup (chooop); *hinchado*

T

tail *n.* neh (neh); *cola, rabo*

take *tr. v.* bisik (BEES-eek); ch'a'ik (CH'AH'-eek); *llevarlo*

take away *tr. v.* hatzik (HAHTZ-eek); *quitarlo*

take care of (care for) *tr. v.* kanantik (KAHN-ahn-TEEK); *cuidarlo*

take out *tr. v.* ho'osik (HOH'-OHS-eek); *sacarlo*

tame *adj.* suuk (soook); *manso*

tangled (in several places) *adj.* so'oso'ok' (SOH'-OH-soh'-ok'); *enredado*

tank *n.* aak'al (AAHK'-ahl); *tanque*

tarantula *n.* chiin wol (CHEEEN wohl); *tarántula*

tarry *in. v.* xáantal (SHÁAHN-tahl); *tardarse, demorarse*

tasty *adj.* ki' (kee'); *sabroso*

tayra (animal, *Tayra barbara*) *n.* saampol (SAAHM-pohl); *oso colmenero, perico ligero*

teach *tr. v.* ka'ansik (KAH'-AHN-seek); *enseñarlo*

teacher *n.* ka'ansah (KAH'-AHN-sah); *maestro*

teat *n.* iim (eeem); *teta*

tell *tr. v.* a'al(ik) (AH'-AHL-[eek]); tzikbatik (TZEEK-bah-TEEK); *decir*

ten *n.* lahun (LAH-hoon) (hypothetical); *diez*

tendon *n.* xiich' (sheeech'); *tendón*

tense *adj.* t'iinil (T'EEEN-eel); *tenso*

testicles *n.* u ye'el toon (oo yeh'-ehl TOOHN); *cojones, testículos*

thank you *phr.* dios bo'otik; (DEE-yohs boh'-oh-TEEK); Sp. + Maya; *¡gracias!*

that *conj.* ka'ah (kah'-ah); *que*

thatched house *n.* xa'anil nah (SHAH'-AHN-eel NAH); *casa de paja*

thatch palm *n.* xa'an (shah'-ahn); *palmo para techo, guano*

that (one) *pron.* lelo' (LEH-loh'); *ése, ésa*

then *adv.* túun (tóoon); *entonces*

there is/there are *adv.* yaan (yaahn); *hay*

there isn't/there aren't *adv.* mina'an (MEE-nah'-ahn); *no hay*

therefore *adv.* le beetik (leh BEEH-teek); *por eso*

there/here it is! *dem.* he'el(a')/(o') (HEH'-EHL-a'/o') *¡aquí/allí está!*

thick *adj.* píim (péeem); polok (POHL-ohk); *grueso, gordo*

thicken *in. v.* su'utal (SOO'-OO-tahl); *espesar*

thickness *n.* poolkil (POOHL-keel); *gordura*

thin *adj.* bek'ech (BEHK'-ehch); *delgado*

thin (paper, clothes) *adj.* haay (haahy); *papel o ropa delgado*

thing *n.* ba'al (bah'-ahl); *cosa*

think *in. v.* tuukul (TOOOHK-ool); *pensar*

think *tr. v.* tuklik (TOOK-leek); *pensarlo*

thirsty *adj.* uk'ah (OOK'ah); *tener sed*

thirteen *n.* óox lahun (óohsh LAH-hoon) (hypothetical); *trece*

this (one) *pron.* lela' (LEH-lah'); *éste, ésta*

thorn *n.* k'i'ix (K'EE'-eesh); *espina*

thought *n.* tuukul (TOOOK-ool); *pensamiento*

three *n.* óox (óohsh); *tres*

three (inanimate things) *adj., pron.* óoxp'éel (ÓOHSH-p'éehl); *tres (cosas)*

three (people or animals, animate things) *adj., pron.* óoxtúul (ÓOHSH-tóool); *tres (personas o animales)*

three times *adv.* óoxpuul (ÓOHSH-poool); *tres veces*

thresh *in. v.* p'uuch (p'oooch); *desgranar*

thresh *tr. v.* p'uchik (P'OOCH-eek); *desgranar*

throat *n.* kaal (kaahl); *garganta*

throb *in. v.* péek (péehk); *palpitarse, moverse*

throw *tr. v.* ch'inik (CH'EEN-eek); *tirar*

throw stones (at) *tr. v.* ch'inik (CH'EEN-eek); *tirar piedras a*

thrush (bird) *n.* pich' (peech'); *tordo (cantor), zorzal (ave)*

thunder *n.* hum cháak (HOOM cháahk); *trueno*

tick (insect) *n.* peech (peehch); *garrapata*

tie *tr. v.* k'axik (K'AHSH-eek); *amarrarlo*

tilt *tr. v.* nixik (NEESH-eek); *inclinarlo*

tilted *adj.* niixil (NEEESH-eel); *inclinado*

time *n.* k'iin (k'eeen); *tiempo*

tire *refl. v.* ka'anal (KAH'-AH-nahl); *cansarse*

tired *adj.* ka'ana'an (KAH'-AH-nah'-ahn); *cansado*

to *prep.* ti' (tee'); *a*

toad *n.* muuch (moooch); *sapo*

toast *adj.* oop' (oohp'); *tostada*

toasted *adj.* pokbil (POHK-beel); *tostado*

tobacco *n.* k'uutz (k'oootz); *tabaco*

to be sure *adv.* he'ele' (HEH'-EHL-eh'); *sí, claro*

today *n.* behla'(e') (BEH-lah'-[eh']); *hoy*

today (earlier) *n.* behla'ak (beh-LAH'-AHK); *hoy anteriormente*

toe *n.* aal ook (AAHL oohk); *dedo de pie*

together *prep.* yéetel (YÉEH-tehl); *con, juntos*

tomato *n.* p'aak (p'aahk); *jitomate, tomate*

to me *prep. phr.* ten (tehn) (contraction of *ti'* and *teen*); *a mí*

tomorrow *n.* sáamal (SÁAH-mahl); *mañana*

tomorrow (day after) *n.* ka'abeh (KAH'-AH-beh); *la mañana siguiente* tongue *n.* ak' (ahk'); *lengua*

tongue (language) *n.* t'aan (t'aahn); *idioma, lengua*

tool *n.* nu'ukul (NOO'-OOK-ool); *instrumento, herramiento, utensilio*

too much *adj.* hach ya'ab (HAHCH yah'-ahb); *mucho, bastante*

tooth *n.* koh (koh); *diente*

toothpick *n.* ch'ilib (CH'EEL-eeb); *palillo de dientes*

tortilla *n.* waah (waah); *tortilla*

totally *adv.* hum puli' (hoom POO-lee'); *totalmente*

toucan *n.* piitor(l)eeyaal (PEEE-toh-r[l]eeh-yaahl); Sp. loanword; *pitoreal*

tough *adj.* chich (cheech); tz'u'uy (TZ'OO'-ooy); *duro, correoso*

town *n.* kaah (kaah); *pueblo, poblacíon*

to you *prep.* he'le' (HEH'-leh'); *a ti/a usted*

to you all *prep.* ti' te'ex (tee' TEH'-ESH); *a ustedes*

trap *n.* peetz' (peehtz'); *trampa*

trash *n.* sohol (SOH-hohl); *basura*

tree *n.* che' (cheh'); *árbol*

trick *tr. v.* kechtik (KEHCH-teek); *embaucarlo*

true *adj.* haah (haah); *verdadero*

trunk *n.* chuun (chooon); *tronco*

truth *n.* haahil (HAAH-eel); *verdád*

turkey (domesticated) *n.* úulum (ÓOO-loom); *pavo*

turkey (oscelated, wild, *Agriocharis ocellata*) *n.* kuutz (koootz); *pavo del monte*

turtle *n.* áak (áahk); *tortuga*

twelve *n.* lahka'a (LAH-kah'-ah) (hypothetical); *doce*

twenty *n.* hun k'áal (HOON k'áahl) (hypothetical); *veinte*

twice *adv.* ka'apúul (KAH'-AH-póool); *dos veces*

twig *n.* ch'ilib (CH'EEL-eeb); *ramita*

twins *pl. n.* k'uho'b (K'OO-hoh'b); *gemelos*

twist *tr. v.* kopik (KOH-peek); *torcer*

two *n.* ka'ah (kah'-ah); *dos*

two hundred *n.* lahun k'áal (LAH-hoon K'ÁAHL) (hypothetical); *doscientos*

two (inanimate things) *adj., pron.* ka'ap'éel (KAH'-AH-p'éehl); *dos (cosas)*

two (people or animals, animate things) *adj, pron.* ka'atúul (KAH'-AH-tóool); *dos (personas o animales)*

two times *adv.* ka'apúul (KAH'-AH-póool); *dos veces*

U

understand *tr. v.* na'atik (NAH'-AH-teek); ohéeltik (oh-HÉEHL-teek); *entenderlo, comprenderlo; reconocerlo, notar*

underwear *n.* eex (eehsh); *calzón*

untidy *adj.* loob (loohb); *desordenado*

untie *tr. v.* wach'ik (WAHCH'-eek); *desatarlo, soltarlo*

until *prep.* aasta (AAHS-tah), tak (tahk); Sp. loanword; *hasta*

until Sunday *prep.* tak domingo (tahk doh-MEEN-goh); Sp. + Maya; *hasta el domingo*

up *adj., adv., prep.* ka'anal (KAH'-AHN-ahl); *arriba*

uproot *tr. v.* t'okik (T'OHK-eek); *arrancarlo*

urinate *in. v.* wiix (weeesh); *orinar*

urine *n.* wiix (weeesh); *orina*

us *1st p. pl. pron.* to'on (toh'-ohn); *nosotros*

use *tr. v.* báaxtik (BÁASH-teek), ch'aik (CH'AH-eek); *usarlo*

used (secondhand) *adv.* asben/asbe'en (AHS-behn/AHS-beh'-ehn); *de medio uso*

used up *adj.* xuupul (SHOOO-pool); xu'upi (SHOO'-OO-pee); *gastarse; gastado*

used up *par.* xu'upi (SHOO'-OO-pee); *se gastó*

useless *in. v.* nuum (nooom); *inútil*

utensil *n.* nu'ukul (NOO'-OOK-ool); *utensilio*

V

value *n.* tohol (TOH-hohl); *valor*

vendor (female) *n.* xkoonol (eesh-KOOH-nohl); *vendedora*

vendor (male) *n.* koonol (KOOHN-ohl); *vendedor*

venison *n.* kéeh (kéeh); *carne de venado*

verge of (on the) *prep.* ta'aytak (TAH'-AHY-tahk); *ya mero, inminente, casí*

very *adv.* hach (hahch); *muy*

very (evaluates quantity) *adv.* sen (sehn); *-ísimo, mucho*

vine *n.* aak' (aahk'); *bejuco*

virgin *n.* suhuy (SOO-hooy); *virgen*

virgin forest *n.* suhuy k'áax (SOO-hooy K'ÁAHSH); *monte virgen (nunca labrada)*

visit *tr. v.* xíimbatik (SHÉEEM-BAHT-eek); *visitarlo*

voice *n.* kaal (kaahl); *voz*
vomit *n.* xeh (sheh); *vómito*
vomit *in. v.* xeh (sheh); *vomitar*
vulture *n.* ch'oom (ch'oohm), kuch (kooch); *zopilote*

W

wait *in. v.* pa'at (pah'-aht); *esperar*
wait for *tr. v.* pa'atik (PAH'-AHT-eek); *esperarlo*
walk *in. v.* xíimbal (SHÉEEM-bahl); *caminar*
walking (on foot) *adj.* wa'bal (WAH'-bahl); *de pie*
wall (of masonry) *n.* pak' (pahk'); *pared de
    mampostería*
want *in. v.* k'áat (k'áaht); taak (taahk); *quiero* (I want);
    querer, tener ganas
warm (luke) *adj.* k'íinal (K'ÉEE-nahl); *tibio*
wart *n.* aax (aahsh); *verruga*
wash *tr. v.* p'o'ik (P'OH'-eek); *lavarlo*
washed *adj.* p'o'a'al (P'OH'-ah'-ahl); *lavado*
washtub *n.* cheem (cheehm); *cuba de lavar*
wasp *n.* xuux (shooosh); *avispa*
water *n.* ha' (hah'); *agua*
wave *in. v.* payk'ab (PAHY-k'ahb); *señalar, señal*
waylay *tr. v.* ch'uktik (CH'OOK-teek); *acecharlo*
we *1st p. pl. pron.* to'on (TOH'-ohn); *nosotros*
wealthy *adj.* ayik'al (ahy-EEK'-ahl); *rico*
weasel *n.* ooch (oohch), sáabin (SÁAH-been); *comadreja*
weave *tr. v.* wak'ik (WAHK'-eek); *tejer*
weed *n.* k'áax (k'áahsh); *yerba*
weed *in. v.* páak (páahk); *desherbar*
weed *tr. v.* páaktik (PÁAHK-teek); *desherbarlo*
weep *in. v.* ok'ol (OHK'-ohl); *llorar*
weigh *tr. v.* p'isik (P'EES-eek); *pesarlo*
weight *n.* aal (aahl); *peso*
well *adv.* ma'alob (mah'-AHL-ohb); *adecuado, bueno*
well *n.* ch'e'en (ch'eh'-ehn), sayap ha' (SAHY-ahp HA');
    pozo, cisterna
west *n.* chik'in (CHEE-k'een); *oeste, occidente, poniente*
wet *adj.* ch'uul (ch'oool); *mojado*
wet (to become) *in. v.* ch'ul chahtal (ch'ool CHAH-
    tahl); *mojarse*
what? *inter.* ba'ax (bah'-ahsh); *¿qué?*
when *conj.* ka'ah (kah'-ah); *cuando*

when (what day)? *inter.* ba'ax k'iin (BAH'-ahsh K'EEEN); *¿cuándo?*

when (what hour)? *inter.* ba'ax oorah (BAH'-ahsh OOHR-ah); *¿cuándo?*

where? *inter.* tu'ux (too'-oosh); *¿dónde?*

which? *inter.* máakalmáak (MÁAHK-ahl-MÁAHK); *¿cuál?*

whip *tr. v.* hatz'ik (HAHTZ'-eek); *azotarlo*

whistle *n.* piito (PEEE-toh); Sp. loanword; *pito*

whistle *in. v.* xuuxub (SHOOO-shoob); *chiflar, silbar*

white *adj.* sak (sahk); *blanco*

white earth (used in mortar) *n.* sahkab (SAHK-ahb); *roca calcárea deleznable, sascab*

white man/woman *n.* tz'uul (tz'oool); *extranjero, ladino*

white woman *n.* xunáan (SHOO-náahn); *extranjera, ladina*

who? *inter.* máaxi' (máahsh-EE'); *¿quién?*

who *pron.* máax (máahsh); *quien*

whoever *pron.* he'e máax (heh'-eh MÁAHSH); *quien*

who knows *adv.* kensa bixi (kehn-sah BEE-shee); *quien sabe*

why? *inter.* ba'ax ten (BAH'-ahsh-tehn); *¿por qué?*

wide *adj.* kóoch (kóohch); *ancho*

wife *n.* atan (AH-tahn); *esposa*

wiggle *in. v.* péek (péehk); *menearse*

wild *adj.* k'o'ox (K'OH'-ohsh); *bravo, salvaje, cimarrón*

wild (animal) *adj.* ba'alche' (BAH'-AHL-cheh'); *animal silvestre*

will *n.* óol (óohl); *ganas*

winch *n.* pechéech (PEH-chéehch); *malacate*

wind *n.* iik' (eeek'); *viento, aire*

wing *n.* xiik' (sheeek'); *ala*

wish *tr. v.* tz'íiboltik (TZ'ÉEEB-ohl-teek); *desearlo*

witch *n.* xwáay (eesh-WÁAHY); *bruja*

with *prep.* ti' (tee'); yéetel (YÉEH-tehl); *en; con*

within *prep.* ichil (EECH-eel); *dentro*

without *adv., prep.* ma' (mah'); xma' (eesh-MAH'); *sin*

wizard *n.* hwáay (ah-wáahy); *brujo*

woman *n.* ko'olel (KOH'-ohl-EHL); xch'úup (eesh-CH'ÓOOP); *mujer*

woman (foreign) *n.* xunáan (SHOO-náahn); *mujer extranjera*

woman (old) *n.* nohoch ko'olel (NOH-hoch koh'-ohl-EHL), xnuuk (eesh-NOOOK); *vieja*

woman (white) *n.* xunáan (SHOO-náahn); *mujer blanca*

won't *adv.* ma'a taan (MAH'-AH taahn); *no*

wood *n.* che' (cheh'); *madera*

word *n.* t'aan (t'aahn); *palabra*

work *n.* meyah (MEH-yah); *trabajo*

work *in. v.* meyah (MEH-yah); *trabajar*

work (rapidly) *adj.* áalkab meyah (ÁAHL-kahb MEHY-ah); *trabajar muy rápido*

world *n.* kaab (kaahb); *mundo*

worm *n.* kaan (kaahn), nok'ol (NOHK'-ohl); *gusano*

wound *n.* loob (loohb), loobil (LOOHB-eel); *herrida, daño*

wrap *tr. v.* to'ik (TOH'-eek); *envolverlo*

wrinkle *tr. v.* ch'ukik (CH'OOK-eek); *arrugarse*

write *in. v.* tz'íib (tz'éeeb); *escribir*

write *tr. v.* tz'íibtik (TZ'ÉEEB-teek); *escribirlo*

writing *n.* tz'íib (tz'éeeb); *escritura*

wrong *adj.* k'eban (K'EH-bahn); *pecado*

Y

yam *n.* iis (eees); *camote*

year *n.* aanyo (AAHN-yoh), ha'ab (hah'-ahb); Sp. loanword; *año*

yell *in. v.* awat (AH-waht); *gritar, dar gritos*

yellow *adj.* k'an (k'ahn); *amarillo*

yes *adv.* haah (haah), he'ele' (HEH'-EHL-eh'); *sí*

yesterday *n.* ho'olheyak (HOH'-ohl-HEH-yahk); *ayer*

you *pron.* teech (teehch); *tú/usted*

youth *n.* xi'ipal (SHEE'-EE-pahl); *joven*

PHRASEBOOK CONTENTS

COMMON WORDS AND PHRASES

Who?
> **Máaxi'?**
> (MÁAH-shee')
> *¿Quién?*

What? Huh?
> **Bixi'?**
> (BEESH-ee')
> *¿Cómo?*

Where?
> **Tu'ux?**
> (too'-oosh)
> *¿Dónde?*

How?
> **Bix?**
> (beesh)
> *¿Cómo?*

When (what day)?
> **Ba'ax k'iin?**
> (BAH'-ahsh K'EEEN)
> *¿Cuándo?*

When (what hour)?
> **Ba'ax oorah?**
> (BAH'-ahsh OOHR-ah)
> *¿Cuándo?*

Why? What for?
> **Ba'axten?**
> (bah'-ahsh-TEHN)
> *¿Por qué?*

Which?
> **Máakalmáak?**
> (MÁAHK-ahl-MÁAHK)
> *¿Cuál?*

How many?
> **Hay túul?**
> (HAHY tóool)
> *¿Cuántos?*

How much does it cost?
> **Bahux u tohol?**
> (BAH-hoosh oo TOH-hohl)
> *¿Cuánto cuesta? ¿Cúal es su precio?*

Ah!
> **An!**
> (ahn)
> *¡Ah!*

no, not, without
> **ma'**
> (mah')
> *no, ni, sin*

never
> **ma'a tech**
> (MAH'-AH tehch)
> *no por puesto*

Not me.
> **Ma' teni'.**
> (mah' TEHN-ee')
> *Yo no.*

COMMON WORDS AND PHRASES

What's that?
> **Ba'ax lelo'?**
> (bah'-ahsh LEH-loh')
> *¿Qué es?*

What is it?
> **Ba'axi'?**
> (BAH'-AHSH-ee')
> *¿Qué es eso?*

I don't know.
> **Ma'in woohli'.**
> (mah'-een WOOHL-ee')
> *No lo sé.*

Speak slowly.
> **T'aneh chaambeel.**
> (T'AHN-eh chaahm-BEEHL)
> *Habla despacio.*

What does that expression mean?
> **Ba'ax u k'aat u ya'alik?**
> (BAH'-AHSH ooh K'AAHT ooh YAH'-
> AHL-eek)
> *¿Qué significa este dicho?*

I don't understand it.
> **Ma' tin na'atik.**
> (mah teen NAH'-AHT-eek)
> *No entiendo.*

a little (quantity)
> **hump'íit**
> (HOOM-p'éeet)
> *un poquito*

COMMON WORDS AND PHRASES

Perfect!
Hach beyo'!
(hahch BEH-yoh')
¡Perfecto!

white person
tz'uul
(tz'oool)
gringo

I am a man.
Wíinken.
(WÉEENK-ehn)
Soy hombre.

I am a woman.
Xch'úupen.
(eesh-CH'ÓOOP-ehn)
Soy mujer.

Watch out! Be careful!
Kanáant a bah(e'ex)!
(KAHN-áahnt ah bah-[EH'-ehsh])
¡Ten cuidado!

May I take a picture here?
Hu' chabal in mentik hump'éel pootooh waye'?
(hooh' CHAH-bahl een MEHN-teek hoom-P'ÉEHL pooh-tooh WAH-yeh')
¿Puedo tomar una foto aquí?

See you tomorrow/until tomorrow.
Tak sáamal.
(tahk SÁAHM-ahl)
Hasta mañana.

Good luck. (Literally, "May it go well with you.")
> **Ka xi'ik teech utzil.**
> (kah SHEE'-EEK teehch ootz-EEL)
> *Que le vaya bien.*

You too.
> **Bey xan teech.**
> (BEHY shahn TEEHCH)
> *Usted también.*

GREETINGS AND POLITE EXPRESSIONS

The Maya generally lack words equivalent to the greetings and polite expressions found in English. "Hello," "how are you?," "please," "thank you," and even the simple affirmation of "yes" all lack counterparts in Maya. Rather, in situations that call for these types of expressions, the Maya equivalent becomes a formulaic and metaphoric response, as in the use of *dios bo'otik* ("God pays it") for "thank you."

Hello.
> **Oola.**
> (OOH-lah)
> *Hola.*

How are you? (General greeting. Literally, "How are things with you?")
> **Bix a beel(e'ex)?**
> (BEESH ah beehl -[EH'-ehsh])
> *¿Qué tal?*

What's going on? (General greeting. Literally, "Where do you go?")
> **Tu'ux ka bin?**
> (too'-oosh KAH been)
> *¿Qué pasa?*

How are you? (General greeting. Literally, "What do you say?")
> **Ba'ax ka wa'alik?**
> (bah'-ahsh kah WAH'-AHL-eek)
> *¿Qué tal?*

Fine, OK.
> **Ma'alob.**
> (mah'-ah-LOHB)
> *Bien.*

(It is) nothing.
> **Mixba'al.**
> (meesh-BAH'-AHL)
> *Nada.*

So-so.
> **Chen beya.**
> (chehn BEHY-ah)
> *Bastante bien.*

Thank you. (Literally, "God pays it," from Sp.
  dios le pagará, "God will pay you.")
> **Dios bo'otik.**
> (DEE-ohs BOH'-OH-teek)
> *Gracias.*

No, God pays it to/for *you* (response to being
  thanked).
> **Ma', dios bo'otik teech.**
> (mah', DEE-ohs BOH'-OH-teek teehch)
> *No, gracias a usted.*

Surely! (Literally, "That's the way it will be.")
> **He'ele'!**
> (HEH'-EH-leh')
> *¡Es cierto!*

Yes, true.
> **Haah.**
> (haah)
> *Sí. Cierto. Ciertamiente.*

GREETINGS AND POLITE EXPRESSIONS

Yes! (Literally, "Like that!")
> **Beyo'!**
> (BEHY-oh')
> *¡Así! ¡Eso!*

Yes! (Literally, "Like this!")
> **Beya'!**
> (BEHY-ah')
> *¡Así! ¡Eso!*

Where are you from? (Literally, "What is your town?")
> **Tu'ux a kaahal?**
> TOO'-OOSH ah KAAH-hahl)
> *¿Cuál es su pueblo?*

Where did you start traveling from? (Literally, "Where did you flee from?"/"Where did you come from?")
> **Tu'ux luk'ech?**
> (TOOH'-OOSH look'-EHCH)
> *¿De dónde venió?*

Where do you come from?
> **Tu'ux a taal?**
> (TOOH'-OOSH ah TAAHL)
> *¿De dónde viene usted?*

What day do you go?
> **Ba'ax k'iin a bin?**
> (BAH'-AHSH k'eeen AH been)
> *¿A qué día se va?*

When will you return?
> **Ba'ax k'iin a suut?**
> (BAH'-AHSH k'eeen ah SOOOT)
> *¿Cuándo regresa?*

GREETINGS AND POLITE EXPRESSIONS

May I approach?
Ka páahtal in natz'ik imbah?
(kah PÁAHT-ahl een NAHTZ'-eek eem-BAH)
¿Puedo cercarme?

Good-bye. (Literally, "May it go to you.")
Tak sáamal.
(tahk SÁAHM-ahl)
A usted(es) . . . (singular/plural)

Good luck. (Literally, "May you go well.")
Ka xi'ik te'ex hatz'utzil.
(kah SHEE'-eek teh'-ehsh HAHTZ'-ootz-eel)
Que le vaya muy bien./Buena suerte.

Likewise. (Literally, "To you.")
Bey xan teech.
(behy SHAHN teehch)
Lo mismo a usted.

May God protect you.
Ka'ah dios kaláanteech.
(Kah'-ah DEE-ohs kah-láahn-TEEHCH)
Que dios le proteja.

NAMES OF PEOPLE AND THINGS

Speakers of Maya generally address each other or their acquaintances by first name, which often derives from Spanish. However, many names of tourists or non-Maya have no equivalent in Spanish, and travelers may find it easiest to adopt a Spanish name for convenience. Many Maya names actually represent nicknames, often in reference to a feature or characteristic of the individual.

the Maya
> **le maayao'obo'**
> (leh MAAH-yah-oh'-ohb-oh')
> *los mayas*

What's your name?
> **Ba'ax a k'aaba'?/Bix a k'aaba'?**
> (BAH'-AHSH ah K'AAHB-ah'/BEESH ah
> K'AAHB-ah)
> *¿Cómo se llama usted?*

John is my name.
> **Hwaan in k'aaba'.**
> (WHAAHN een K'AAHB-ah')
> *Juan es mi nombre.*

What is that called?
> **Bix u k'aaba' lelo'?**
> (BEESH ooh K'AAHB-ah' LEH-loh')
> *¿Cómo se llama ése?*

NAMES OF PEOPLE AND THINGS

Does it have a Maya name also?
> **Yaan hump'éel k'aaba ich maayah
> bey xan?**
> (yaahn HOOM-p'éehl K'AAHB-ah eech
> MAAH-yah behy SHAHN)
> *¿Hay un nombre maya también?*

Isn't there any Maya word?
> **Mina'an t'aan ich maayah?**
> (MEEN-ah'-ahn t'aahn eech maah-YAH)
> *¿No hay una palabra en maya?*

How is _____ said in Maya?
> **Bix _____ u ya'ala'al ich maayah?**
> (beesh _____ oo YAH'-AHL-ah'-ahl
> eech maah-YAH)
> *¿Cómo se dice _____ en maya?*

Can _____ be said in Maya?
> **Hu' beeta'al _____ u ya'la'al ich
> maayah?**
> (hoo' beeht-ah'-al _____ oo
> YAH'L-ah'ahl eech maah-YAH)
> *¿Se puede decir _____ en maya?*

Which expression is better, _____ or
_____?
> **Ba'ax t'aan u maasil utz, _____ wáah
> _____?**
> (BAH'-AHSH t'aahn oo MAAHS-eel OOTZ,
> _____ wáah _____)
> *¿Cuál dicho es mejor, _____ o
> _____?*

What does that expression mean?

Ba'ax u k'áat u ya'alik le t'aano'?

(BAH'-AHSH oo k'áaht oo YAH'-AHL-eek
   leh T'AAHN-oh')

¿Qué quiere decir ese dicho?

TIME

Many Spanish loanwords have made their way
into Maya as expressions of time, including *dyae*
for *día* (day) and *anyo* for *año* (year). Maya uses
Spanish forms for all of the days of the week and
months of the year as well, but these can take the
Maya suffix *-ak* to indicate the *previous* day or
month (for example, *sábadoak* "last Saturday").

today
> **behla'e'**
> (BEH-lah'-eh')
> *hoy*

yesterday
> **ho'olheyak**
> (HOH'-OHL-heh-yahk)
> *ayer*

tomorrow
> **sáamal**
> (SÁAH-mahl)
> *mañana*

every day (also means "over and over, regularly")
> **sansamal**
> (sahn-SAHM-ahl)
> *cada día*

the day after tomorrow
> **ka'abeh**
> (KAH'-AH-beh)
> *el día después de mañana*

the day after the day after tomorrow
óoxbeh
(ÓOHSH-beh)
el día después del día después de mañana

now (Sp. + Maya)
be'ooráa'
(beh'-OOHR-áah')
ahora

right away, just now
be'ooriita'
(beh'-oohr-EEET-ah')
ahorita

all the time, all day
lah k'iinil
(lah K'EEEN-eel)
todo el tiempo, todo el día

morning
ha'atzkab k'iin
(hah'-ahtz-kahb K'EEEN)
mañana

dusk
áak'abtal
(áahk'-AHB-tahl)
anochecer

night
áak'ab
(ÁAHK'-ahb)
noche

last night
> **áabak**
> (ÁAH-bahk)
> *la noche pasada*

last year
> **anyoak** (from Spanish *año*)
> (ahn-YOH-ahk)
> *el año pasado*

late (in the day)
> **ka'ka't(e')**
> (KAH'-kah't-[e'])
> *al rato, un poco después, más tarde*

long ago
> **úuchih**
> (ÓOOCH-ee)
> *anteriormente*

early
> **hatzkab k'iin**
> (hahtz-kahb K'EEEN)
> *temprano, la mañana*

earlier
> **ka'achih**
> (KAH'-AH-chee)
> *antes*

tomorrow (see you tomorrow)
> **sáamal**
> (SÁAH-mahl)
> *mañana*

until tomorrow
tak sáamal
(tahk SÁAH-mahl)
hasta mañana

until another day
tu láak' k'iin
(too LÁAHK' k'eeen)
hasta un otro día

What day? When?
Ba'ax k'iin?
(BAH'-AHSH k'eeen)
¿Cuál día? ¿Cuándo?

What time (what hour)? (Sp. + Maya)
Ba'ax oorah?
(BAH'-AHSH oohr-ah)
¿Cuál tiempo?

What time (generally)? (Sp. + Maya)
Ba'ax tyempoh?
(BAH'-AHSH TYEHM-poh)
¿Cuál tiempo?

AGE AND STATUS

Maya speakers show respect to elders by referring to them as "large" or "great" (*nohoch*). Otherwise the Maya refer to individuals by name.

gentleman
> **yuum**
> (yooom)
> *caballero, señor*

lady
> **xunáan**
> (SHOO-náahn)
> *dama*

his/her age
> **u ha'abil**
> (oo HAH'-AHB-eel)
> *el edad de él/ella*

old man
> **nohoch máako'**
> (noh-hohch MÁAH-koh')
> *viejo*

> **nohoch wíinik**
> (noh-hohch-WÉEEN-eek)
> *viejo*

old woman
> **nohoch ko'olel**
> (noh-hohch KOH'-OHL-ehl)
> *vieja*

grandfather (literally, "great father, great man")
nohoch taat(ah)
(NOH-hohch TAAHT-[ah])
abuelo

old people (in general) (literally, "the great
people")
le nukuch máako'obo'
(leh noo-kooch MÁAHK-oh'-ohb-oh')
viejos (gente grande)

American/European tourists (literally, "white
odors")
sak boko'ob
(sahk BOHK-oh'-ohb)
olores blancos, gringos

black people (African-Americans)
boxo'ob
(BOHSH-oh'-ohb)
negros

male (foreigner)
tz'uul
(tz'oool)
hombre, extranjero

female (foreigner)
xunáan
(SHOO-náahn)
mujer, extranjera

his lady (wife of a white man)
u xunáan
(oo SHOO-náahn)
su mujer (esposa de un extranjero)

How old are you?
> **Hayp'el a ha'abil?**
> (HAHY-p'ehl ah HAH'-AHB-eel)

> or

> **Hay p'éel aanyos yaan teech?**
> (HAHY p'éehl AAHN-yohs yaahn TEEHCH)
> *¿Cuántos años tiene?*

girl, young woman
> **xch'úupal**
> (eesh-CH'ÓOOP-ahl)
> *muchacha*

PERSONAL RELATIONSHIPS

Except for the terms for siblings, relationship terms tend to be exclusively Spanish or a Mayanization of Spanish. For example, the Maya generally express the concept of "family" or "relative" by the term *pamíilyah*, a Mayanization of Spanish *familia*. More distant relatives are referred to by name. Nationality terms are also exclusively Spanish loanwords, modified by the more or less lilting accent and emphasis of the Maya language and by differences of tone and stress.

mother
> **na'**
> (nah')
> *madre*

father
> **taat(ah)**
> (TAAHT-[ah])
> *padre*

wife
> **atan**
> (AH-tahn)
> *esposa*

my wife
> **in watan**
> (een WAH-tahn)
> *mi esposa*

your wife
> **a watan**
> (ah WAH-tahn)
> *su esposa*

John's wife
> **u yatan Juan**
> (oo YAH-tahn WHAAHN)
> *la esposa de Juan*

grandfather (great father)
> **nohoch taat(ah)**
> (NOH-hohch TAAHT-[ah])
> *abuelo*

grandmother
> **chiich**
> (cheeech)
> *abuela*

son/daughter
> **paal**
> (paahl)
> *hijo/a*

children
> **paalo'ob**
> (PAAHL-oh'-ohb)
> *hijos*

twins
> **k'uho'b**
> (K'OO-hoh'b)
> *gemelos*

elder sister
> **kiik**
> (keeek)
> *hermana mayor*

elder brother
suku'un
(SOO-kooh'-oon)
hermano mayor

younger brother/sister
íitz'in
(ÉEETZ'-een)
hermano/hermana menor

true sibling
láak'tzil
(LÁAHK'-tzeel)
hermano(a) verdadero(a)

relative (aunt, uncle, cousin)
láak'
(láahk')
miembro de familia

all my relatives
tuláakal in láak'tzilo'ob
(tooh-LÁAHK-ahl een láahk'-tzeel-OH'-
    OHB)
toda mi familia

she/he doesn't recognize me
ma' tu k'ahóoltikeni'
(mah' too k'ah-óohl-tee-KEHN-ee')
ella/él no me conoce

my younger stepbrother/sister
in mahan íitz'in
(een MAH-hahn ÉEETZ'-een)
mi hermanastro/a

my stepmother
in mahan maamah
(een MAH-hahn maah-MAH)
mi madrastra

friend (Sp.)
áamigoh
(aáh-MEE-goh)
amigo

I'm getting married.
Tun tz'o'okol in beel.
(toon TZ'OH'-OHK-ohl een beehl)
Voy a casarme.

LODGING

Lodging on the Yucatán Peninsula ranges from posh tourist resorts to campsites on the beaches. However, accommodations off the beaten path in the many Maya villages remain nearly nonexistent, and often the traveler must find a local family to stay with or find a place to hang a hammock in the schoolhouse or community buildings (always ask permission). Services and amenities at public hotels, motels, and hostels vary widely depending on the quality and on the price the traveler is willing to pay for a room. Often Maya families will rent unused thatch huts for slinging hammocks, and a variety of establishments exclusively feature these types of shacks for the budget traveler.

Can I spend the night in this town?
Hu' beeta'al in p'áatal ti' le kaahala'?
(hoo' beeh-TAH'-AHL een P'ÁAHT-ahl tee'
  leh KAAH-HAHL-ah')
*¿Puedo quedarme en esta pueblo por la
  noche?*

Where can I hang my hammock?
Tu'ux yaan in ch'uyik in k'áan?
(TOO'-OOSH yaahn een CH'OOY-eek een
  K'ÁAHN)
¿Dónde puedo colgar mi hamaca?

Can I hang my hammock here?
Ku p'áatal in ch'uyik in k'áan waye'?
(koo' P'AAHT-ahl een CH'OOY-eek een
  k'áahn WAHY-eh')
¿Puedo colgar mi hamaca aquí?

Do you want to hang your hammock here?
A k'áat wáah ch'uyik in k'áan waye'?
(ah K'ÁAHT wáah CH'OOY-eek een k'áahn
WAHY-eh')
¿Quiere colgar su hamaca aquí?

I stayed here.
P'áaten waye'.
(P'ÁAH-tehn WAH-yeh')
Me quedé aquí.

Are you awake yet?
Ahal nahech?
(AH-hahl NAH-hehch)
¿Está usted despierto?

The man is snoring.
Tun nóok le máako'.
(toon NÓOHK leh MÁAHK-oh')
El hombre está roncando.

It's noisy.
Yaan ya'ab huum.
(YAAHN yah'ahb HOOOM)
Hace mucho ruido.

RESTAURANT SERVICE, FOOD, AND DRINK

Opportunities to show off your knowledge of Maya rarely arise in fast-paced tourist destinations on the Yucatán Peninsula such as Cancún or Mérida, except when dealing with service personnel and guides. These jobs are some of the only ones generally open to Maya speakers. By far, many more occasions open up along country roads and in small villages, where a stop at a *comedor* (small restaurant) or food stall will reward your effort at communicating in Maya.

Restaurant Service

breakfast
> **uk'ul**
> (OOK'-ool)
> *desayuno*

dinner, food
> **o'och**
> (oh'-ohch)
> *cena, comida*

meal
> **hanal, hanlil, o'och**
> (HAHN-ahl, HAHN-leel, OH'-ohch)
> *comida*

eat, eating
> **hanal** (*in.*), **haantik** (*tr.*)
> (HAHN-ahl, HAAHN-teek)
> *comer, comerlo*

Let's go eat.
> **Ko'ox hanal.**
> (koh'ohsh HAHN-ahl)
> *Vamos a comer.*

What do you want to eat?
> **Ba'ax tak a haantik?**
> (BAH'-AHSH tahk ah HAAHN-teek)
> *¿Qué quiere comer?*

And you?
> **Kux teech?**
> (KOOSH teehch)
> *¿Y usted?*

Give me _____.
> **Tz'a teen _____.**
> (TZ'AH teehn)
> *Por favor, dáme _____.*

I've already asked for it.
> **Tz'o'ok in k'áatik.**
> (TZ'OH'-OHK een K'ÁAHT-eek)
> *Ya ordené./Ya lo pedí.*

I'm very hungry.
> **Hach wi'iheen.**
> (HAHCH WEE'-EE-heehn)
> *Tengo mucho hambre.*

Are you hungry?
> **Wi'iheech?**
> (WEE'-EE-heehch)
> *¿Tiene hambre?*

Please bring me a (cup of) coffee.
Tas teen hump'éel boxha'/kaapeh.
(TAHS teehn HOOMP'-éel bohsh-
HAH'/KAAH-peh)
Por favor, traígame un café.

Do you want to eat now?
K'aat a hanal beyoorah?
(K'AAHT ah HAHN-ahl behy-OOHR-ah)
¿Quiere usted comer ahora?

Have you got any _____ today?
Yaan teech _____ behla'e'?
(YAAHN teehch _____ BEH-lah'-eh')
¿Tiene usted _____ hoy?

There isn't any _____.
Mina'an
(MEE-nah'-ahn)
No hay _____.

Please bring me (a) _____.
Tas teen (hump'éel) _____.
(TAHS teehn hoom-P'ÉEHL _____)
Por favor, traígame _____.

The _____ are fresh.
Hach áak' le _____ o'.
(HAHCH áahk' leh _____ oh')
Los _____ están frescos(as).

I'd like some _____.
In k'áat _____.
(EEN k'áaht _____)
Quiero algo de _____.

Would you like (some) _____?
> **A k'áat _____?**
> (ah K'ÁAHT _____)
> *¿Quiere usted algo de _____?*

Just a little (more). (Sp. + Maya)
> **Chéen hump'íit (maas).**
> (CHÉEHN HOOM-p'éeet [maahs])
> *Solo un poco (más).*

That's enough/too much.
> **Ya'ab.**
> (yah'-ahb)
> *Es suficiente./Es demasiado.*

Please fill it up.
> **Chupeh.**
> (CHOOP-eh)
> *Llénalo, por favor.*

very tasty
> **hach ki'**
> (hahch KEE')
> *muy sabroso*

I like it/[It's] good to my eye.
> **Utz tin wich.**
> (ootz teen WEECH)
> *Me gusta.*

My meal is burned.
> **Eelel in wo'och.**
> (EEHL-ehl een WOH'-OCH)
> *Está quemado mi comida.*

Anything else?
U maasil?
(oo MAAHS-eel)
¿Algo más?

Do you want anything else?
A k'áat wáah u maasil?
(ah K'ÁAHT wáah oo MAAHS-eel)
¿Quiere algo más?

That's all.
Che'en lelo'.
(cheh'ehn LEH-loh')
Es todo.

I'm done eating.
Tz'o'ok in hanal.
(TZ'OH'-OHK een HAHN-ahl)
Ya terminó de comer.

Take it away (please).
Biseh.
(BEES-eh)
Tómalo, por favor.

Good eating! (Bon appetit!)
Hach ki' a hanal!
(hahch kee' ah HAHN-ahl)
¡Buen provecho!

Maya Cuisine

Many of the modern world's favorite foods origi-
nated in the New World among Native American
civilizations, long before Columbus and the first
European explorers reached America. How would

the rest of the world fare without corn, beans, tomatoes, potatoes, chili, squash, chocolate, peanuts, vanilla, and other food plants first domesticated in North and South America? Imagine pizza without tomato sauce, to give only one example.

The Maya themselves evolved a distinctive cuisine from many of the New World's domesticates, inventing specialty dishes that today can be found in the restaurants of Mérida and Cancún as well as other locations on the Yucatán Peninsula. Black beans, chili, tortillas, and boiled maize products have become all-important to the Maya diet. Most famous of all is the Maya "pit bar-b-que," cooked in an underground cavity called a *piib*, which features pork and chicken baked in banana leaves and marinated in sour orange juice, garlic, and red achiote sauce. However, the Maya's diet rarely includes meat other than chicken, largely for economic reasons and because of a decline in wild game due to loss of forest habitat. Similarly, the Maya consume few dairy products, and they derive most of what they drink from ground maize in the form of *sa'* (atole, or cooked corn gruel) and *k'eyem* (pozole, or uncooked corn gruel). Of course, soft drinks (Coca Cola or other sodas) can be found everywhere.

fried chicken
> **tzahbil kaax**
> (TZAHB-eel KAAHSH)
> *pollo frito*

pit bar-b-que pork
> **pibil k'éek'en**
> (PEEB-eel K'ÉEH-k'ehn)
> *cochinita pibil*

pit bar-b-que chicken
pibil kaax
(PEEB-eel KAAHSH)
pollo pibil

roast pork
pok chúuk
(POHK chóook)
carne de chochinito asado

grilled fish in annatto marinade (marinade based
around a red food dye)
tikin xik'
(TEE-keen sheek')
pescado a la parilla

Maya egg rolls (crumbled hard-boiled eggs
wrapped in tortilla and dipped in pumpkin
seed sauce)
papa tz'ules
(PAH-pah TZ'OOL-ehs)
*rollo relleno de huevos duras con salsa
de calabaza*

corn mush, posol
k'eyem
(K'EH-yehm)
pozole

gravy, thick sauce
k'óol
(k'óohl)
salsa

chili black sauce
box k'óol
(bohsh-K'ÓOHL)
salsa negra con chili

black bean sauce
> **k'óobil bu'ul**
> (K'ÓOHB-eel BOO'-OOL)
> *salsa de frijoles negro*

eggs Motul-style (named after the town of Motul
in the state of Yucatán)
> **u he'il Motul**
> (oo HEH'-eel moh-TOOL)
> *huevos motuleños*

honey beer (fermented from honey and flavored
with tree bark)
> **báalche'**
> (BÁAHL-cheh')
> *balche*

Food

avocado
> **oon**
> (oohn)
> *aguacate*

banana
> **ha'as**
> (hah'-ahs)
> *plátano*

beans
> **bu'ul**
> (boo'-ool)
> *frijoles*

beef
> **u bak'el wakax**
> (ooh BAHK'-ehl wah-KAHSH)
> *carne de res*

bitter
> **k'áah**
> (k'áah)
> *amargo*

chicken
> **kaax**
> (kaahsh)
> *pollo*

chili
> **iik**
> (eeek)
> *chile*

corn
> **(i)xi'im**
> ([ee]-shee'-eem)
> *maíz*

eggs
> **he'o'ob**
> (HEH'-oh'-ohb)
> *huevos, blanquillos*

fish
> **kay**
> (kahy)
> *pescado*

guava
> **pichi'**
> (PEECH-ee')
> *guava*

honey
> **kaab**
> (kaahb)
> *miel*

hot sauce (literally "dog's nose")
> **xni' peek'**
> (SHNEE' peehk')
> *salsa picante*

meat
> **bak'**
> (bahk')
> *carne*

meat (fresh)
> **áak' bak'**
> (ÁAHK' bahk')
> *carne fresca*

orange (sweet)
> **chiinah**
> (CHEEE-nah)
> *naranja dulce*

paca (*Cuniculus paca*)
> **haleb**
> (HAHL-ehb)
> *tapescuintle*

papaya
> **puut**
> (pooot)
> *papaya*

peccary (collared) (*Pecari tajacu*)
> **kitam**
> (KEE-tahm)
> *jabalí, coche del monte*

pumpkin
>**k'úum**
>(k'óoom)
>*calabaza*

salt
>**ta'ab/ta'abik**
>(tah'-ahb/TAH'-AHB-eek)
>*sal*

sour
>**pah**
>(pah)
>*agria*

sour orange tree/sour orange
>**pak'áal**
>(PAHK'-áahl)
>*naranjo/a agrio(a)*

spicy, hot
>**páap**
>(páahp)
>*picante, caliente*

squash
>**k'úum**
>(k'óoom)
>*calabaza*

sugar
>**asukaar** (Sp.)
>(ah-SOO-kaahr)
>*azúcar*

sweet orange (common orange)
chiinah pah
(CHEEE-nah PAH)
naranja dulce

sweet stuff (sugar, etc.)
ch'uhuk
(CH'OO-hook)
dulce

tomato
p'aak
(p'aahk)
tomate

tortilla, bread
waah
(waah)
tortilla

tortilla chips
tzahbil waah
(TZAHB-eel waah)
chips (de tortilla)

venison
kéeh
(kéeh)
venado

Drink

For the most part what the Maya drink when thirsty is some kind of maize gruel, usually atole (*sa'*), which is a cooked gruel, or pozole (*k'eyem*), which is uncooked. They also rely heavily on drinking some type of soft drink (*Kooka*, or Coca Cola). Beer and commercial cane liquor play a large role in everyday life, and the latter serves as an indispensible item used in religious ritual, especially as an offering to the gods. As always, whenever traveling in Latin American countries, avoid fresh or tap water or any products that contain water that may be contaminated.

I'm thirsty.
Hach uk'ahen.
(hahch oo-K'AH-hehn)
Tengo sed.

Are you thirsty?
Uk'aheech (wáah)?
(oo-K'AH-eehch [wáah])
¿Tiene usted sed?

water
ha'
(HAH')
agua

cold water
síis ha'
(séees HAH')
agua fría

hot water
chokoh ha'
(CHOH-koh HA')
agua caliente

corn gruel
sa'
(SAH')
atole

corn gruel made from fresh maize (green corn)
áak' sa'
(ÁAHK' sah')
atole de maíz tierno, atole nuevo

corn mush drink, uncooked maize gruel, posol
k'eyem
(K'EH-yehm)
pozole

orange juice
k'aab chiina
(k'aahb CHEEE-nah)
jugo de naranja

beer
seerbeesah
(seehr-BEEH-sah)
cerveza

get drunk
káaltal
(KÁAHL-tahl)
emborracharse

Is there Coca Cola? How much for the Coca Cola?
Yaan hump'éel Kooka?
(yaahn hoom-p'éehl KOOHK-ah)
¿Hay refrescos? ¿Hay Coca Cola? ¿Cuánto cuesta?

Shopping

For the most part, situations on the Yucatán Peninsula where people speak Maya and that involve "shopping" in the Western sense are extremely rare. Apart from encounters with small village stores and itinerant vendors who approach tourists on the street, the chance to use Maya when buying something will arise only occasionally, and usually only in the larger towns and cities. Some shop employees at tourist centers may speak Maya, but for the most part such employees will speak Spanish or even English. Try out your Maya in these situations and after a moment of awkwardness while your listener adjusts to your accent, you will no doubt be very well received.

When asking for a certain number of items, bear in mind that, in Maya, counted objects take "numerical classifiers" depending on the type of object in question. For example, with inanimate objects you use the classifier -*p'éel*, with "long things" -*tz'íit*, and with people and animals -*túul*.

Where do they sell _____?
 Tu'ux ku ko'onol _____?
 (TOO-OOSH koo KOH'-OHN-ohl

  _____)
  ¿Dónde se vende _____?

I'm looking for (a) _____.
 Tin kaxtik (hump'éel) _____.
 (teen KAHSH-teek [hoom-P'ÉEHL]

  _____)
  Estoy buscando _____.

Where is _____?
> **Tu'ux yaan _____?**
> (TOO'-OOSH yaahn _____)
> *¿Dónde está _____?*

How many?
> **Hay túul?**
> (HAHY tóool)
> *¿Cuántos?*

How much does it cost?
> **Bahux u tohol?**
> (BAH-hoosh oo TOH-hohl)
> *¿Cuánto cuesta? ¿Cuál es su precio?*

price
> **tohol**
> (TOH-hohl)
> *precio*

Please give me _____.
> **Tz'ah teen _____.**
> (TZ'AH teehn)
> *Por favor, dáme _____.*

(very) too expensive
> **hach ko'oh**
> (hahch KOH'-OH)
> *(muy) demasiado caro*

Is that all?
> **Chéen lelo'?**
> (chéehn LEH-loh')
> *¿Es todo?*

Something else? (Sp. + Maya)
U maasil?
(oo MAAHS-eel)
¿Algo más?

Clothing

dress
nook'
(noohk')
ropa

dress (native woman's)
iipil
(EEEP-eel)
huipil

hat
p'ok
(p'ohk)
sombrero

hat (straw)
xa'anil p'ook
(SHAH'-AHN-eel P'OOHK)
sombrero de paja

pants
eex
(eehsh)
pantalón

shawl
booch'
(boohch')
rebozo

underwear
> **eex**
> (eehsh)
> *calzón*

Toiletry

comb
> **xáache'**
> (SHÁAHCH-eh')
> *peine*

Books and Stationery

book, paper
> **hu'un**
> (hoo'-oon)
> *libro*

TRANSPORTATION AND TRAVEL

The Yucatán Peninsula abounds in public transportation, ranging from long-distance buses connecting to other parts of the country to *colectivos* or minibuses on shorter local runs. Yucatán boasts two international airports, one at Mérida and the other at Cancún, as well as rail transportation up the west coast of Yucatán from the interior of the country. Most frequently, the Maya use buses and *colectivos*, and the most common of all means of transportation, walking. Some Maya own livestock such as horses, mules, or burros. The Maya refer to all of these forms of transportation almost exclusively in Spanish, varying the pronunciation of words in terms of the distinctive Maya accent and emphasis on stress and tonality.

Note that some of the following examples take *k* where action is habitual or *t* where action is ongoing or progressive. For example, *tin bin* means "I am going (right now)" whereas *kin bin* means "I go (everyday, etc.)."

Where are you going?
>**Tu'ux ka bin?**
>(too'-oosh KAH been)
>*¿Adónde va?*

Where are you going? (*pl.*)
>**Tu'ux ka bine'ex?**
>(too'-oosh KAH been-EH'-ehsh)
>*¿Adónde van?*

me too
> **beyxan teen**
> (BEHY-shahn teehn)
> *yo también*

Do you want to get in/on?
> **A k'áat na'akal (e'ex)?**
> (AH k'áaht NAH'-AHK-ahl-[eh'-ehsh])
> *¿Quiere subirse?* (sg.)/*¿Quieren subirse*
> *ustedes?* (pl.)

I'm only going to _____.
> **Chéen ti' _____ kin bin.**
> (CHÉEHN tee' _____ KEEN been)
> *Me voy sólo hasta _____.*

we are approaching
> **táan k natz'ik k bah**
> (táahn k nahtz'-eek k BAH)
> *estamos acercandole*

Where do you get out?
> **Tu'ux ka wéemel(e'ex)?**
> (TOO-OOSH kah WÉEHM-ehl-[eh'-ehsh])
> *¿Dónde se baja?*

there
> **te'elo'**
> (TEH'-EH-loh')
> *allí*

here
> **te'ela' (waye')**
> (TEH'-EH-lah' [wahy-eh'])
> *aquí*

Where does this road/highway go?

Tu'ux ku bin le béeha'/u caareteerah?

(TOO'-OOSH koo been leh BÉEH-hah'/
oo caah-reh-TEEH-rah)

¿Por dónde va éste camino/carretera?

let's go

ko'one'ex

(KOH'-ohn-EH'-ehsh)

vamos

I'm looking for _____ to photograph.

**Tin kaxtik _____ utia'al in meent
pootoohs.**

(teen KAHSH-teek _____ oo-tee-AH'-
AHL een meehnt pooh-toohs)

*Estoy buscando _____ para tomar
fotos.*

May I take a picture here/of you/of you all?

**Hu' chabal in meent hump'éel pootooh
waye' ti'/teech/te'ex'?**

(hoo' CHAHB-ahl een meehnt hoom-
P'ÉEHL pooh-tooh WAHY-eh'
tee'/teehch/teh'-ehsh)

*¿Puedo tomar una foto aquí/de usted/
de ustedes?*

Are there any_____ around here?

Yaan _____ waye'?

(yaahn _____ WAHY-eh')

¿Hay algunos _____ cerca de aquí?

Where can you see them?

Tu'ux ku yila'al o'ob?

(TOO'-OOHSH koo YEEL-ah'-ahl oh'-ohb)

¿Dónde se puede verlos?

Just wait here a bit.

Pa'ateh waye' hump'íit.
(PAH'-AH-teh WAHY-eh' hoom-P'ÉEET)
Espérate aquí un poco.

all over the world

yóok'ol le kaabo'
(YÓOHK'-ohl leh KAAHB-oh')
en todo el mundo

Directions

east

lak'in
(LAH-k'een)
este, oriente

north

xaman
(SHAH-mahn)
norte

south

nohol
(NOH-hohl)
sur

west

chik'in
(CHEE-k'een)
oeste, occidente, poniente

HEALTH AND PERSONAL HYGIENE

Health services on the Yucatán Peninsula consist for the most part of health clinics and doctors in private practice. Hospitals can be found in the larger cities. Most doctors and nurses tend to be non-Maya because of educational and economic factors, although the situation has been changing in more recent years. Services in most types of health facilities will generally be conducted in Spanish. Maya villages have their folk-healers, or *curanderos* (Spanish), who treat problems with ritual performances and a variety of herbal and mineral remedies.

In general, avoid fresh water or products made of water of any type, unless the product has undergone pasteurization. Be extremely wary of fresh vegetables that may have been washed or rinsed in water. Water may be safe in the larger tourist hotels, but never count on it. It is better to refrain from drinking fresh tap water, or water from rivers or streams. Drink only purified bottled water and ice.

As anywhere in the world, avoid uncooked or undercooked meats, especially poultry. For the most part, no specific vaccinations are recommended for Mexico, but bear in mind that malaria still lurks in some areas of the Maya world, especially the jungles. Exercise caution when consuming shellfish, which can spoil quickly in the tropical climate.

If you suspect any illness more serious than the flu or a cold, seek professional medical help immediately. Prolonged diarrhea can lead to dehydration, and probably indicates the presence of parasites, most likely in the form of amebic dysentery. Other serious problems can include food poisoning, severe sunburn (especially in beach areas and the Maya ruins), and forms of hepatitis. Because of the intense sunlight in Yucatán, keep yourself hydrated and maintain a steady salt intake. Remember that traveling in itself can deplete your energies.

cold medicine
> **tz'aak se'en**
> (tz'aahk SEH'-ehn)
> *medicina para catarro*

corn (on foot)
> **t'aaham**
> (T'AAH-hahm)
> *callo*

cough (dry)
> **se'en**
> (seh'-ehn)
> *toser*

doctor, physician
> **htz'aak/xtz'aak**
> (ah-TZ'AAHK/eesh-TZ'AAHK)
> *doctor; médico(a)*

finger
> **u yaal a k'ab**
> (oo YAAHL ah K'AHB)
> *tu dedo del mano*

foot, leg
> **ook**
> (oohk)
> *pie, pierna*

headache
k'i'inam pool
(K'EE'-EE-nahm poohl)
dolor de cabeza

illness
k'oha'anil
(K'OH-hah'-ahn-EEL)
enfermedad

injury, wound, accident
loob
(loohb)
daño, herida, accidente

medicine
tz'aak
(tz'aahk)
medicina

needle
púutz'
(póootz')
aguja

pain
yaah
(yaah)
dolor

penis
toon
(toohn)
pene

pregnant
>**yo'om**
>(yoh'-ohm)
>*embarazada*

sick
>**k'oha'an**
>(K'OH-ah'-ahn)
>*enfermo*

toe
>**u yaal a wook**
>(ooh YAAHL ah woohk)
>*tu dedo del pie*

vomit
>**xeh**
>(sheh)
>*vómito, vomitar*

wart
>**aax**
>(aahsh)
>*verruga*

weight
>**aal**
>(aahl)
>*peso*

Useful Phrases

John is sick.
>**K'oha'an Juan.**
>(K'OH-hah'-ahn WHAAHN)
>*Juan está enfermo.*

I am sick.
K'oha'aneen.
(K'OH-hah'-ahn-eehn)
Estoy enfermo(a).

I'm recovering from illness.
Tin ch'aik in wool.
(teen CH'AH-eek een WOOHL)
Estoy recuperando.

I'm very tired.
Hach ka'na'aneen.
(hach kah'-nah'-AHN-eehn)
Estoy muy cansado(a).

inside me
ichil ti' teen
(EECH-eel tee' TEEHN)
dentro de mí

I'm going to take a bath.
Tin bin ichkíil.
(TEEN been EECH-kéeel)
Voy a bañarme.

My throat is sore.
Ma' kal in kaal.
(MAH' kahl een KAAHL)
Tengo dolor de garganta.

I'm cold.
Ke'eleen.
(KEH'-EHL-eehn)
Tengo frío.

I'm hurt.
> **Ki'impaheen.**
> (kee'eem-PAH-heehn)
> *Se me heridó.*

I have a stomachache.
> **Hach yah in nak'.**
> (hahch yah een NAHK')
> *Me duele la barriga.*

The lady is pregnant.
> **Yo'om le ko'olelo'.**
> (yoh'-ohm leh KOH'-oh-LEH-loh')
> *La mujer está embarazada.*

Do you have a cold?
> **Yaan teech se'en?**
> (yaahn teehch SEH'-ehn)
> *¿Tiene catarro?*

WORK

As the most common occupation among the Maya of the Yucatán Peninsula, farming meets the basic needs of the Maya family and supplies its staples. Almost every Maya owns and works a cornfield either by himself or with other family members or friends. Generally confined to a small plot of land, called a *milpa* (singular) in Spanish and *kool* in Maya, the farmer (*milpero* or *koolnáal*) clears away the jungle brush during the dry season by burning it off. He then plants his triumvirate of agricultural produce—corn, beans, and squash—by jabbing the soil with a "digging stick" (*lóob*) and dropping seeds inside the hole. He does this in time for the growing season, which coincides with the summer rains.

Probably the second most common occupation among the Maya is the selling of Maya arts and crafts, which provides a mainstay for local economies. Generally, the Maya occupy lesser positions in the hotel and tourist industries, working for the most part as bellhops, maids, maintenance workers, and in other service positions. However, many guides at local tourist attractions tend to be bilingual in Maya and Spanish.

bean
> **bu'ul**
> (BOO'-ool)
> *frijol*

bean (lima)
> **iib**
> (eeeb)
> *frijol de lima*

brush, weed, forest, jungle
k'áax
(k'áahsh)
yerba, monte, bosque

corn
xi'im
(shee'-eem)
maíz

corn (ear of)
nal
(nahl)
elote

diligent
utz u meyah
(OOTZ oo MEH-yah)
diligente

fire
k'áak'
(k'áahk')
fuego

harvest (*in.*)
hooch
(hoohch)
cosechar

harvest (*tr.*)
hochik
(HOHCH-eek)
cosecharlo

knife blade (his) (Maya + Sp.)
u yeh kuchiiyoh
(oo yeh koo-CHEEE-yoh)
filo de cuchillo

seed (for sowing maize)
i'inah
(EE'-EE-nah)
semilla para sembrar maíz

seed (in general)
neek'
(neehk')
semilla, pepita

seedbed (raised)
ka'anche'
(KAH'-AHN-cheh')
plantío elevado

seeder (stick for planting)
xúul
(shóool)
coa, sembrador

seeds (pumpkin/squash)
sikil
(SEEK-eel)
pepita de calabaza

squash
k'úum
(k'óoom)
calabaza

squash seeds
sikil
(SEEK-eel)
pepita de calabaza

Useful Phrases

He works quickly.
> **Áalkab u meyah.**
> (ÁAHL-kahb oo MEHY-ah)
> *Trabaja muy de prisa.*

I want to visit a milpa. (Literally, "I want to take a
   walk to the milpa.")
> **Tak in xíimbal ich kool.**
> (tahk een SHÉEEM-bahl eech KOOHL)
> *Quiero visitar una milpa.*

Can you show me your milpa?
> **He'el beeta'al a we'esik teen a koole'?**
> (heh'ehl BEEHT-AH'-ahl ah WEH'-ehs-eek
>   teehn ah KOOHL-eh')
> *¿Puede enseñarme su milpa?*

When do you burn the field?
> **Ba'ax k'íin a tóokik le koolo'?**
> (BAH'-AHSH k'éeen ah TÓOHK-eek leh
>   KOHL-oh')
> *¿Cuándo va a quemar la milpa?*

When do you plant?
> **Ba'ax k'íin a pak'al?**
> (BAH'-AHSH k'éeen ah PAHK'-ahl)
> *¿Cuándo va a sembrar la milpa?*

You can't carry that.
> **Lelo' ma' tu páahtal kuchik.**
> (LEH-loh' mah' too PÁAH-tahl KOOCH-eek)
> *Eso no lo puede cargar.*

I am done/ready.
Tz'o'okeen.
(TZ'OH'-OHK-eehn)
Estoy terminado/listo, se cabó.

I'm going hunting.
Tin bin tz'oon.
(Teen been TZ'OOHN)
Voy a cazar.

cut firewood
xotik si'
(SHOH-teek SEE')
cortar leña

ENTERTAINMENT

The sport of choice throughout Latin America is soccer (*fútbol*), and this is no less true in the Maya areas. Soccer terms in use among the Maya are usually borrowed or derived from Spanish. However, as North American games such as baseball and basketball increase in popularity, the Maya have been adopting native terms to express the necessary vocabulary.

Do you want to play _____?
> **Ak'áat _____ báaxtik?**
> (AHK'-áaht _____ BÁAHSH-teek)
> *¿Usted quiere jugar _____?*

I've got to look for it.
> **Yaan in kaxtik.**
> (Yaahn een KAHSH-teek)
> *Debo buscarlo.*

John won. (Sp. derivative)
> **Gáanarnah Juan.**
> (gáah-NAHR-nah WHAAHN)
> *Juan ganó.*

I lost. (Sp. derivative)
> **Perdernaheen.**
> (pehr-dehr-NAH-heehn)
> *Yo perdí.*

run
> **áalkab**
> (ÁAHL-kahb)
> *correr*

I am running.
> **Kin wáalkab.**
> (keen WÁAHL-kahb)
> *Corro.*

to beat (in a game)
> **p'uuch**
> (p'oooch)
> *batear*

hit with a stick (baseball)
> **p'uchik**
> (P'OOCH-eek)
> *golpear con palo*

to pitch
> **chiin**
> (cheeen)
> *tirar*

catch
> **chukik**
> (CHOOK-eek)
> *alcanzarlo*

Do you want to dance with me?
> **Ak'áat wáah ok'ot tin we'ehel?**
> (ahk'-áaht WÁAH ohk'-oht teen
>   WEH'-eh-hehl)
> *¿Usted quiere bailar conmigo?*

Weather and Natural Phenomena

Because it lies within the tropics at almost sea level, the whole of the Yucatán Peninsula experiences only two seasons—wet and dry. Generally beginning towards the end of February and ending in late May or early June, the dry season can turn the country into a veritable desert. Cactus often clings to the crest of overgrown and ruined buildings of the ancient past, while vegetation diminishes in height toward the drier north until it becomes essentially scrub forest—a far cry from the true rain forests along the peninsula's southern base. From June to January, storms subject the peninsula to frequent and often torrential downpours.

As a tropical region that defines the western limit of the Caribbean basin, the Yucatán Peninsula experiences regular hurricanes and other powerful storms that rage from out at sea to the east. Much less frequently, earthquakes rock the country, although earthquakes tend to center in the more volcanic areas of Guatemala to the south.

cloud
> **mu(n)yal**
> (MOO[N]-yahl)
> *nube*

cloudy
> **nóokoy**
> (NÓOHK-ohy)
> *nublado*

WEATHER AND NATURAL PHENOMENA

cold
> **ke'el**
> (keh'-ehl)
> *frío*

dark (fairly)
> **ée'ho'ch'e'en**
> (ÉEH'-ho'-CH'EH'-ehn)
> *medio oscuro*

earth tremor (Literally, "The earth is shaking.")
> **tun kíilbal lu'um**
> (toon KÉEEL-bahl loo'-oom)
> *tiembla de tierra*

great wind (literally, "hard wind")
> **chich iik'**
> (CHEECH eeek')
> *viento grande/fuerte*

hot, humid
> **k'íilkab**
> (K'ÉEEL-kahb)
> *hace calor, húmedo*

hurricane, cyclone
> **chak ik'al**
> (chahk EEK'-ahl)
> *huracán*

morning star, Venus
> **xnuk ek'**
> (EESH-nook EHK')
> *estrella de la mañana, Venus*

muggy
> **k'as k'íilkab**
> (k'ahs K'ÉEEL-kahb)
> *medio húmedo*

north wind
> **xaman ka'an**
> (SHAH-mahn KAH'-ahn)
> *viento del norte*

rain
> **cháak/ha'**
> (cháahk/hah')
> *lluvia*

star
> **eek'**
> (eehk')
> *estrella*

storm
> **chichiik'**
> (CHEECH-eeek')
> *tempestad, temporal, huracán*

sun
> **k'iin**
> (k'eeen)
> *sol*

sunset
> **bin ka ak'abtal**
> (been kah ahk'-AHB-tahl)
> *anochecer*

warm, hot
> **chokoh**
> (CHOHK-oh)
> *tibio, caliente*

wind
> **iik'**
> (eeek')
> *viento, aire*

Useful Phrases

It's not hot.
> **Ma' chokohi'.**
> (mah' chohk-OH-hee')
> *No hace calor.*

I am cold.
> **Ke'eleen.**
> (KEH'-EHL-eehn)
> *Tengo frío.*

become dark
> **ée'ho'ch'e'ental**
> (ÉEH'-hoh'-CH'EH'-EHN-tahl)
> *oscurecer*

It's getting dark.
> **Tun yée'ho'ch'e'ental.**
> (toon YÉEH'-ho'-CH'EH'-ehn-tahl)
> *Se oscurece.*

It's raining.
> **Tun k'áaxal ha'.**
> (toon K'ÁAHSH-ahl HAH')
> *Está lloviendo.*

It rained yesterday.
K'áax ha' ho'olheyak.
(K'ÁAHSH hah' hoh'-ohl-HEH-yahk)
Ayer llovía.

The sky is clear (of objects).
Háanil le ka'ano'.
(HÁAHN-eel leh KAH'-AHN-oh')
Está despejado el cielo.

The wind is strong.
Táah k'a'an iik'.
(táah K'AH'-AHN eeek')
El viento es muy fuerte.

The sky is changing.
Tun k'eex le ka'ano'.
(toon K'EEHSH leh KAH'-AHN-oh')
Está cambiando el tiempo.

The north wind is coming.
Tun taal le xaman ka'ano'.
(toon taahl leh SHAHM-ahn KAH'-ahn-oh')
Viene el viento del norte.

NUMBERS

one *n.* hun (hoon); *uno*

one (person or animal) *adj., pron.* huntúul (hoon-TÓOOL); *un(a) (persona o animal)*

one (inanimate thing) *adj., pron.* hump'éel (hoomp'-ÉEHL); *un(a) (cosa)*

one (long thing) *adj., pron.* huntz'íit (hoon-TZ'ÉEET); *un(a) (cosa larga)*

one (tree) *adj., pron.* hunkúul (hoon-KÓOOL); *un(a) (árbol)*

two *n.* ka'ah (kah'-ah); *dos*

two (persons or animals) *adj., pron.* ka'atúul (KAH'-AH-tóool); *dos (personas o animales)*

two (inanimate things) *adj., pron.* ka'ap'éel (KAH'-AHP'-éehl); *dos cosas*

two times *adv.* ka'apúul (KAH'-AH-póool); *dos veces*

three *n.* óox (óohsh); *tres*

three (persons or animals) *adj., pron.* óoxtúul (ÓOHSH-tóool); *tres (cosas)*

three (inanimate things) *adj., pron.* óoxp'éel (ÓOHSHP'-éehl); *tres (personas o animales)*

three times *adv.* óoxpuul (ÓOHSH-poool); *tres veces*

four *n.* kan (kahn); *cuatro*

four (persons or animals) *adj., pron.* kantúul (kahn-TÓOOL); *cuatro (personas o animales)*

four (inanimate things) *n.* kamp'éel (kahm-P'ÉEHL); *cuatro (cosas)*

five *n.* ho' (hoh'); *cinco*

(Numbers above "five" hypothetical only; actual words unknown. Maya speakers use Spanish numbers.)

six *n.* wak (wahk); *seis*
seven *n.* uk (ook); *siete*
eight *n.* waxak (WAH-shahk); *ocho*
nine *n.* bolon (BOH-lohn); *nueve*
ten *n.* lahun (LAH-hoon); *diez*
eleven *n.* buluk (BOO-look); *once*
twelve *n.* lahka'a (LAH-kah'-ah); *doce*
thirteen *n.* óox lahun (óohsh LAH-hoon); *trece*
fourteen *n.* kan lahun (kahn LAH-hoon); *catorce*
fifteen *n.* ho' lahun (HOH' LAH-hoon); *quince*
twenty *n.* hun k'áal (HOON k'áahl); *veinte*
forty *n.* ka' k'áal (KAH' k'áahl); *cuarenta*
sixty *n.* óox k'áal (ÓOHSH k'áahl); *sesenta*
eighty *n.* kan k'áal (KAHN k'áahl); *ochenta*
one hundred *n.* ho' k'áal (HOH' k'áahl);
    cien, ciento
two hundred *n.* lahun k'áal (LAH-hoon K'ÁAHL);
    doscientos
four hundred *n.* hun bak (HOON bahk);
    cuatrocientos
eight hundred *n.* ka' bak (KAH' bahk);
    ochocientos
eight thousand *n.* hun pik (hoon PEEK);
    ocho mil